"BY THEIR MAJESTIES' COMMAND"

THE HOUSE OF HANOVER
AT THE LONDON THEATRES, 1714–1800

Harry William Pedicord

London
The Society for Theatre Research
1991

To Kate and Meg Schleifer

First published 1991
by The Society for Theatre Research
c/o The Theatre Museum
1 e Tavistock Street, London WC2E 7PA

© Harry William Pedicord

ISBN 0 85430 050 3

Printed in Great Britain by
E. & E. Plumridge Ltd., Linton, Cambridge

CONTENTS

Abbreviations used in the Summary Tables,
Annex, etc. are explained on p.46

ILLUSTRATIONS AND GENEALOGIES

PLATE 1. 'A Stage Box in London'   *frontispiece*
A water-colour by John Nixon (*fl.* 1784-1815), amateur actor and painter
with a name for theatrical caricature. Prior to coming into the possession
of the Garrick Club the picture was owned by Sir Henry Irving. So far as is
known, it has never before been reproduced.

The caricature purports to show King George III and Queen Charlotte
in a theatre box. The date is probably of the very late 1780's. The occasion
is an invented one. While extracts from Handel's oratorio *Solomon* were
much performed in the 1780's and 1790's, Kane O'Hara's adaptation
from Molière, *The Two Misers,* was less frequently aired with at the most one
or two appearances a year between 1787-90, and according to *The London
Stage Pt.5* the two works were never billed together. The titles on the
playbills in the picture are clearly satirical. The name 'Solomon' was
ironically applied to George III from the time of the American revolution,
when he was blamed for the loss of the colonies. Here 'Solomon' may also
be a cruel reference to the king's bout of porphyria, 1788-89, diagnosed at
the time as insanity. The 'Misers' barb may be aimed more at Queen
Charlotte, whose meanness was a subject of gossip, than at George,
though the slur may have survived from the 1760's when servants were
disgruntled by economies in the royal household; with this resonance, the
satire would bite even more deeply if the picture were to have been
painted after the king's dismissal in March 1789 of Household officers
who had supported the Prince of Wales in the recent regency crisis.

Although it is unflattering to their Majesties, the caricature reinforces
our understanding of how hugely George III enjoyed himself at the
theatre.

(Published by kind permission of the Garrick Club and E.T. Archives.)

PLATE 2.   'The Horrid Assassin...at Drury Lane Theatre'   p.61
This is one of at least two engravings rushed out to illustrate the attempted
assassination of King George III by James Hadfield at Drury Lane
Theatre. The episode is fully described in a contemporary report (see
Annex, entry for 15 May 1800). Errors in the engraving's caption may be
due to the publisher's desire for haste in an effort to pre-empt his
competitors.

(Reproduced by courtesy of the Trustees of the British Museum.)

GENEALOGICAL TABLES

FOREWORD

British theatre scholarship owes a great debt to our colleagues across the Atlantic, not least for their painstaking work in recording performances. No theatre scholar would wish to be without *The London Stage 1660-1800,* published in five parts in eleven volumes, under various editors, by the Southern Illinois University Press at Carbondale, 1960-68. This remarkable calendar of performances, with commentary, has provided a basis for many secondary studies, of which this book is one.

Its author, Harry William Pedicord, is also an American, though well known to many members of the Society for Theatre Research through his long period of residence in London. Professor Pedicord's previous publications include *The Theatrical Public in the Time of Garrick* and a magisterial edition of Garrick's plays. His interest in the attendance of royalty at the London theatres led him to compile his own calendar of command performances and others attended by the Hanoverian royal family. From this stemmed the analytical study which forms the body of this work, and its annex of comment and contemporary reportage. We are glad to be able to publish it as a contribution to the understanding of the place of royal patronage in the arts, a field which remains as important today as it ever was.

IAN HERBERT
Chairman, Publications
August, 1991   *The Society for Theatre Research*

PREFACE

Notice of an appearance by the Royal Family at an eighteenth-century London theatre was usually given in a letter from the Lord Chamberlain's Office to the proprietors one or two days in advance of the visit. Management invariably caused the announcement to be printed on the large bills put up around the city, on the house playbills, and so advised the newspapers of the day. Such notices usually guaranteed increased attendance by an audience that included not only the Royals and their entourage from the Court, but also people of fashion intent on being seen in the royal presence, and a considerable number of commoners taking the opportunity to see their monarch and members of his family at close range.

The doors of the theatres were opened at 5.0 pm and the performance began at 6.0 pm. Some time after 5.30 the royal carriage arrived at a private entrance near the stage door, and a proprietor greeted the notables with a candelabrum with which he lighted the King and Queen to the royal box ante-room at pit level. The King's box was situated on the left-hand side of the auditorium, with the Prince of Wales's box on the right side. (Later in the century King George III had the royal box elevated to adjoin the first tier of the regular boxes.)

At his Majesty's first appearance from the ante-room the entire audience rose and applauded, as the King bowed to the assembled spectators. Then followed the entrance of the Queen and the rest of the Royal Family, bowing to the King and then to the house. After this brief ceremony the play commenced.

At the end of the performance the King stood bowing in acknowledgement of the applause of the audience and withdrew, followed by the remaining Royals clutching their white satin playbills. The proprietor then appeared in the passage with his candelabrum and lighted the way to the carriages for their return journey to the palace.

In this study, all details of Command Performances and other nights of royal attendance have been taken from the volumes of *The London Stage 1660-1800,* the indispensable record of stage history in the eighteenth century. Titles of plays, operas, and other entertainments are usually given in the abbreviated form used by the editors of that work, quoted from playbills and newspaper advertisements. Where appropriate I have added the names of authors, adapters, librettists, and composers, with the dates of composition, to assist the reader in estimating the royal taste in plays and operas of the sixteenth and seventeenth centuries as compared to the works of eighteenth-century contemporaries.

A few words of caution! This sampling of royal entertainment is in no sense an historical study of the theatre. Those interested in such information should consult the volumes by Allardyce Nicoll and other historians listed in the bibliography. Furthermore, the survey is of attendance in London alone. Since these royal visits have been analysed reign by reign, personages attending will be found repeated in different chapters. In chapter three and elsewhere we encounter certain confusion as to royals with identical names. I have been forced to rely on identification of the different royals (such as the Dukes of Gloucester and Cumberland, or successive Princes of Wales) by their birth-and-death dates, or by the use of an excessive number of baptismal names. As Shakespeare's plays were mutilated many times by later alterations, I have omitted dates for his plays, excepting important alterations such as Garrick's.

The analysis in this study makes no claim for absolute accuracy. While care has been taken in its compilation, some unnoticed errors of calculation, or of transcription from *The London Stage 1660-1800,* may remain. Additional theatrical intelligence is to be found in the newspapers and reports of the time beyond what the editors of *The London Stage* have been able to incorporate; any such is outside the scope of the present work, founded as it is solely on the record in *The London Stage.* The interpretation of announcements in playbills and advertisements is a matter of some ambiguity, as the editors of *The London Stage* themselves warn: for example, a Command Performance may have been advertised, but not, in the event, attended; the advertised play may have been changed at no notice; royal family members may have attended a performance unheralded or incognito. Some inconsistencies of this kind have come to light. Others, we can be certain, have not. As always, specialist scholars doing original research will need to return to primary sources and come to their own conclusions. But to them, as to the non-specialist reader, this is offered as a study in which the evidence, the tables, and the findings can be taken as a general guide to an area of interest and significance. There is still work to do on the royal patronage of the arts. As this goes to press, news comes of a paper that can be expected to make a valuable contribution, 'King George I, the Haymarket Opera Company, and the *Water Music*' by Donald Burrows and Robert D. Hume. This is proposed for publication in *Early Music* later in 1991. It makes use of important new information in the Hanover archives.

I wish to acknowledge the kind permission of Southern Illinois University Press and its director Kenny Withers for extensive quotation from the work of Emmett L. Avery, Arthur H. Scouten, George Winchester Stone, Jr., and Charles Beecher Hogan in *The London Stage Parts 2,3,4 and 5*. My thanks also to Professor Edward A. Langhans and Professor Kalman A. Burnim; to the British Museum, the Garrick Club and E.T. Archives for photographic permission; to (now, sadly) the late Dr. Geoffrey Ashton for first drawing to attention the Garrick Club picture formerly owned by Sir Henry Irving and here reproduced, as frontispiece, for the first time, and to Dr. Ashton and Dr. John Clarke for their help with its exegesis; to the staffs of the British Library and Mr. Ian Willison, the Folger Shakespeare Library; to Mr. Ian Herbert, Chairman of the Publications sub-committee of the Society for Theatre Research, and especially to Mr. Derek Forbes, the editor of my manuscript; and to Mr. George Speaight and Professor Arthur H. Scouten for many helpful suggestions along the way.

HARRY WILLIAM PEDICORD

GENEALOGICAL TABLE 1

Pedigree and Children of King George I

GEORGE LEWIS (often spelt LOUIS), 1660-1727:

son of Sophia, 1630-1714, Electress of Hanover and grand-daughter of King James I of England (King James VI of Scotland), who with her line was appointed eventual successor to the British throne by Act of Settlement 1701.

George Lewis married (1682) Sophia Dorothea of Brunswick-Lüneburg-Zell (often spelt Celle), 1666-1726, who in 1694 was imprisoned in Ahlden Castle for the rest of her life following her association with Count von Königsmark, and is sometimes referred to as the Princess of Ahlden.

The marriage was annulled in 1694.

George Lewis became Elector of Hanover in 1698.

Upon the death of the British Queen Anne, two months after his mother's death, George Lewis succeeded to the British throne.

He reigned as King George I of Great Britain and Ireland 1714-1727, the first British king of the House of Hanover.

Children of King George I and Sophia Dorothea

1. GEORGE AUGUSTUS, 1683-1760, Duke of Cambridge
   Prince of Wales 1714-1727
   m. Caroline of Brandenburg-Anspach
   reigned as King George II 1727-1760

2. SOPHIA DOROTHEA, 1688-1757
   m. Frederick William I, King of Prussia

Chapter I

THE REIGN OF GEORGE I, 1714-27

'Hail mighty George! auspicious smiles thy Reign,
Thee long we wish'd. Thee at last we gain.'

Ecstatic verses greeted George Lewis, Elector of Hanover, when he made his tardy arrival at Greenwich on 30 September 1714 to become George I of England. George Lewis was 54 years old at the time of his coronation on Wednesday, 20 October. He was accompanied by his 31-year-old son, George Augustus, his son's wife, Caroline of Anspach, and their four children, Frederick Lewis, Anne, Amelia, and Caroline. These mature royals and their children were to support English theatres in a fashion unknown since the days when Charles II restored the playhouses. William and Mary, and Anne, had shown little interest in the stage or the opera house. Queen Anne considered public theatricals to be too bawdy for her taste and certainly inimical to her beloved Church of England. Then, too, she had been in constant pain throughout her brief reign and confined her amusements for the most part to card games, teas, and the delights of beautiful gardens. Her obesity obliged her to be moved on chairs or by pulleys, making attendance at the public theatres virtually impossible. It is not surprising, therefore, that during her reign, beyond five performances at St. James's Palace (most of them in celebration of her birthday),[1] only two public performances were commanded and four others offered for the entertainment of state guests.[2]

With the arrival of the Hanoverians, however, theatre managers, their companies, and the public at large became aware of the great value of royal patronage in terms of the box-office,[3] the social scene, and the taste of the times. Today we often tend to neglect these nights of the royal presence in the playhouse because we are uncertain as to just what was meant by a 'Command Performance' in the eighteenth century. If we take it for granted that the term implies a royal patron, we soon discover performances so advertised without a single member of the Royal Family gracing the production. At other times a prompter's note will inform us: 'Benefit for ye Author put up by the Prince's command but he did not come.'[4] Most confusing, perhaps, is to encounter (what we might have expected all along) the suggestion that the Lord Chamberlain had a hand in selecting performances to be enjoyed by royalty.

> 'As the taste of the Royal Family is well known to be equal to the delight they take in encouraging genius, it is, we presume, the Lord Chamberlain that so frequently orders, for their entertainment, a hash of old Pantomimes, which even children cannot relish more than once.'[5]

What, then, are we to make of the term 'Command Performance'? Since no convincing evidence has yet appeared, I am inclined to steer a middle course. While there is no explanation for the absence of royalty when such a presence has been indicated on the day's bill, we must assume that the Lord Chamberlain's Office would consult the royals as to particular entertainments they wished to see. In the end, it is my intention to treat all 'Command Performances' as representative of the taste of the Royal Family and to show how these mature Germans patronized the English stage of their times.

Let us begin with His Majesty King George I. It is not so strange that a man of 54, whose native language was German (although he spoke French in a tolerable fashion) should have difficulties in speaking English. It is probable that he understood English but seldom ventured to speak it. Nevertheless, according to the record in *The London Stage Part 2* on which my analysis is based, he was to be found at the theatres of London on one hundred and thirty-one nights, at comedies and farces, pantomimes, opera and musical concerts, to be seen by his subjects, to be entertained, to encourage actors, musicians, writers, and managements, and to absorb what he could of the English tongue. He even enjoyed taking his grandchildren, Princesses Anne, Amelia, and Caroline, to the opera or pantomime (nine or ten times recorded) and occasionally to the play at Drury Lane and Lincoln's Inn Fields or at Court.[6] Often he visited public theatres *incognito*, especially the opera, where 'instead of appearing there in state, he usually went in a sedan-chair, accompanied by his Turkish servants, instead of lords and grooms in waiting, and sat in the box of the Duchess of Kendal'[7] - 'where his presence was not observed by, and was often unknown to the audience'.[8]

Fifty-five of his evenings were devoted to twenty-six operas, his favourites being: *Pyrrhus and Demetrius* (Swiney-Armstrong-Haym-Scarlatti), six nights; *Hydaspes* (Cicognini-Mancini), *Rinaldo* (Hill-Handel), *Lucius Verus* (Zeno-Haym), *Amadis* (de la Motte-Heidegger-Handel), *Otho* (Haym-Handel), four nights each; *Wenceslaus* (Zeno-Humphreys), *Titus Manlius* (Unknown), *Radamistus* (Haym-Handel), *Astartus* (Zeno-Pariati-Rolli), *Cleartes* (Unknown), *Mutius Scaevola* (Mattei-Buononcini-Handel), *Alexander* (Rolli-Handel), two nights each. There were thirteen other operas he heard but once - *The Island Princess, Arminius, Floridante, Ernelinda, Numitor, Griselda, Coriolanus, Flavius, Pharnaces, Julius Caesar, Rodelinda, Elisa, Scipio,* the compositions of Purcell, Handel, Ariosti, Buononcini, Haym, and several unknown composers. It will be noted that five of these were Handel operas - *Floridante, Flavius, Julius Caesar, Rodelinda,* and *Scipio.*

Seventy-one nights were given to stage plays at Drury Lane, the King's Theatre, Lincoln's Inn Fields, and the Haymarket, but only ten of these were attended by the King more than once: namely *Lo Spirito Folletto* (three nights); Shakespeare's *The Tempest, Henry VIII, Julius Caesar, The Merry Wives of Windsor; Le Furbarie Per Vendetta;* Wycherley's *The Country Wife;* Crowne's *Sir Courtly Nice;* Colley Cibber's *Love's Last Shift;* Vanbrugh's *The Relapse* (two nights each). During his reign George I witnessed twenty-four comedies, two historical plays of Shakespeare, two tragedies, and forty-three other pieces of farce, pantomime, and spectacular diversion. His favourite playwrights included: Shakespeare, six performances; Dryden, four performances; Colley Cibber, four performances; Vanbrugh, Crowne, Fletcher, Wycherley, two performances each.

Although the individual actor's contract specified his benefit night and its relative position in the seasonal calendar,[9] the King was often disposed to make a benefit night a 'Command Performance' and was present that evening as a royal patron. Thus George I honoured actors and musicians for fourteen benefit nights, nine at the King's Theatre, four at Drury Lane, and one at Lincoln's Inn Fields. Performers so honoured were: Mrs. Robinson (formerly Mrs. Turner), a musician who was honoured no less than five times; and Antonio Bernacchi (King's Theatre) and Mrs. Santlow (Drury Lane) twice each. Other artists had one evening each - Benedetti Baldassari, 'Signora Diana' and 'Signora Victoria' at the King's Theatre, Mrs. Booth and Mrs. Oldfield at Drury Lane. For the benefit of the French comedians at Lincoln's Inn Fields in 1718 the King presented the company with the sum of one hundred guineas,[10] and when the Italian troupe, sponsored by the Duke of Montague and Richmond, appeared at the King's Theatre in 1726-27 the record indicates that he attended no less than thirty-three performances.

George I especially enjoyed spectacular and fabulous productions such as the entertainment called *Apollo and Daphne* (Theobald-Galliard, 1726) which was formally introduced by an actor in the character of Cupid being flown to the royal box at Lincoln's Inn Fields to deliver to His Majesty a 'Book of the Entertainment.'[11] The Italians at the King's Theatre in 1726 also scored with such elaborate productions as *Arlequin Prince by Enchantment, The Greatest Glory of a Prince, The Enchanted Island of Arcadia, Diana's Madness, Le Furbarie Per Vendetta, Il Matrimonie Disturbate,* and *Lo Spirito Folletto.*

Unlike his father, who favoured opera because he knew little English, George Augustus, Prince of Wales, had an excellent grounding in the classics and could converse decently in French, Italian, or English. We find him attending the English theatres one hundred and eighty-six times to his father's one hundred and thirty-one. With his wife, the accomplished Caroline of Anspach, he commanded sixty-seven performances, and alone he commanded or was present on one hundred and five further evenings. Indeed, it was on the theatrical scene that the violent animosity between father and son was made so painfully public.

The Prince grew up hating his father. Initially it was because of the King's brutal treatment of the Prince's mother, Sophia Dorothea, imprisoned for thirty-two years in the Castle of Ahlden for her affair with Count von Königsmark. In Hanover and again in England the prince was treated with contempt by George I, who refused to allow his son any serious responsibilities of state. George Augustus retaliated by establishing his own more brilliant court during the summer of 1716 at Hampton Court, an effective gathering of the opposition party. The current rift in the Whig party, due to the dismissal of Lord Townsend and the resignation of Sir Robert Walpole, brought many politicians to cultivate George Augustus and Princess Caroline. In December 1717 the Prince and Princess of Wales were expelled from the palace, and early in 1718 they established themselves at Leicester House, and at Richmond during the summers of 1718-1720.[12]

On 31 May 1718 *Read's Weekly Journal* commented: 'We hear the famous Mr. Pinkethman is building a handsome Playhouse at Richmond, for the Diversion of the Nobility and Quality that attend the Court of their Royal Highnesses; and will begin to play there soon after Whitsuntide, and shew the fine musical Picture he has prepar'd of the Royal Family....' Meanwhile, the *Original Weekly Journal* (30 August 1718) informed the public that 'the King hath order'd the Comedians of the Theatre Royal in Drury Lane to perform at Hampton-Court, during his Majesty's stay there, for which Service they are to be allow'd 100 £ extraordinary each Night they act.' The King had ordered a theatre to be erected at his own expense in the Great Hall at Hampton-Court,[13] and before the summer ended seven command performances had been given. Colley Cibber tells us that a warrant of November 1718 for these performances shows expenses incurred by the Drury Lane Company to have amounted to £374 1s. 6d., and adds that George I made the company a present of an additional £200.[14] The heated rivalry continued through the following year until the father and son were eventually 'reconciled' and together attended a performance of *Radamistus* on 11 May 1720. During the quarrel the Prince of Wales attended thirty-one performances to his father's eighteen at the public theatres.

During the family dispute it is interesting to note that the King and the Prince took care not to appear at the same theatre on the same evening. If the King selected an opera, the Prince was to be seen at Drury Lane or Lincoln's Inn Fields. While George I attended only two performances by the French comedians at the King's Theatre and Lincoln's Inn Fields in 1718-19, George Augustus and Caroline commanded nine nights in French. On the other hand, after their reconciliation they commanded a mere five nights for the Italian comedians (1726-27) at Lincoln's Inn Fields and the King's Theatre, while George I commanded a total of thirty-three performances. The record is similar to that established in the 1714-15 season, during which the royal trio first attended London theatres - the King eleven times, the Prince and Princess of Wales forty-nine times - when the family attended to learn English and were reminded of the fact that Louis XIV had made the theatre fashionable in Paris.

Denied most responsibilities, George Augustus became an avid theatregoer and attended one hundred and eighty-six performances. Like his father, the Prince enjoyed the opera (for forty-three performances) and favoured particularly: *Rinaldo* (Hill-Handel) six nights; *Lucius Verus* (Zeno-Haym) four nights; *Radamistus* (Haym-Handel), *Rodelinda* (Haym-Handel), *Hydaspes* (Cicognini-Mancini), *Otho* (Haym-Handel), *Amadis* (Heidegger-Handel), *Arminius* (Unknown), two nights each. Only one night was devoted to such operas as *Pyrrhus and Demetrius, Wenceslas, Sirce, The Island Princess, Pharnaces, Elisa, Julius Caesar, Scipio,* and *Camilla.* Once again the popular composer was Handel, with nine operas (nineteen nights); others were Haym, Mancini, Scarlatti, Buononcini, Bannister, Galliard, and an unknown.

The Prince commanded his theatre in English for the most part. He preferred comedy to tragedy (one hundred and two nights of comedy to twenty-six of tragedy), his favourites being: *The Man of Mode* (Etherege), six nights; *The Rover* (Mrs. Behn), *Marriage A-la-Mode* (Dryden), *The Old Batchelor* (Congreve), *Sir Courtly Nice* (Crowne), *The Relapse* (Vanbrugh), *The Way of the World* (Congreve), *Jane Shore* (Rowe), *Venice Preserv'd* (Otway), three nights each; *The Stratagem* and *The Constant Couple* (Farquhar), *The Amorous Widow* (Betterton), *Rule a Wife and Have a Wife* (Fletcher), *The Chances* (Fletcher-Buckingham), *Bartholomew Fair* and *The Alchemist* (Jonson), *The Provok'd Wife* (Vanbrugh), *Wit Without Money* (Fletcher), *The Double Gallant* (C. Cibber), *The Pilgrim* (Fletcher), *Don John; or The Libertine Destroy'd* (Shadwell), *Cato* (Addison), *Macbeth* (Shakespeare-Davenant-Dryden), *The Indian Emperor* (Dryden), *Aurengzebe* (Dryden), and *The Fatal Constancy* (Sir Hildebrand Jacob), two nights each.

The Prince and Princess of Wales were present as royal patrons on eighteen benefit nights designated as command performances, fifteen at Drury Lane, one at the King's Theatre, and two at Lincoln's Inn Fields. Actors who had set their benefit dates according to contract were honoured by such royal patronage and included: Mrs. Porter (seven), Mrs. Oldfield (three), Pinkethman, D'Urfey, Mills, Norris, and Shaw (one each); 'Pierrot' and John and Charles Rich at Lincoln's Inn Fields (one each). All this patronage by royalty and quality constricted the managers' choice of repertoire. In 1717-18, for example, at least one hundred and twenty-eight performances were either command performances or bespoke by society persons.

Other members of the Royal Family attending the theatres were Anne, Princess Royal, and her younger sisters Princess Amelia and Princess Caroline. There is no record of the presence of the Princes Frederick Lewis or William Augustus until after their father's accession to the throne as George II, and the Princesses Mary and Louisa were still too young at the time. But in 1715, at the ages of 6 and 4, the Princesses Anne and Amelia were taken to the opera twice to hear Handel's *Rinaldo*. Two years later they were at Drury Lane to see Colley Cibber's

Love's Last Shift, and the following summer at Hampton Court to see *The Stratagem* and *Henry VIII* as guests of their grandfather. In 1719 they were joined by a younger sister, Princess Caroline, aged 6, for a series of pantomimic entertainments at the King's Theatre. By the season of 1725-26 the three daughters were to be found at five evenings at the opera (see note 6). It is evident that their elders took an interest in their education in the arts and guided their gradual absorption into the theatrical scene.

SUMMARY OF ATTENDANCE, 1714-27

(See p.46 for explanation of abbreviations)

THE ROYAL FAMILY AT THE THEATRES AND OPERA, 1714-27

	DL	LIF	K'S	HAY	HC	RI	SF
George I	20	9	93	1	8	0	0
George Augustus and Caroline, Prince and Princess of Wales	111	19	47	3	0	5	1
Anne, Princess Royal	1	1	13	0	2	0	0
Princess Amelia	1	1	11	0	2	0	0
Princess Caroline	1	1	9	0	2	0	0
	134	31	173	4	14	5	1

TYPES OF ENTERTAINMENTS ON ROYAL ATTENDANCE NIGHTS, 1714-27

	C	T	F	HP	OP	PA/ENT
George I	30	2	5	4	55	39
George Augustus and Caroline, Prince and Princess of Wales	102	26	11	5	43	16
Anne, Princess Royal	3	0	4	1	18	0
Princess Amelia	3	0	4	1	8	0
Princess Caroline	3	0	4	1	6	0

The reign of George I ended on 14 June 1727. The record in *The London Stage Pt.2* shows that the Royal Family had made three hundred and sixty-two appearances at opera and stage plays and entertainments — one hundred and seventy-three at the King's

Theatre, one hundred and thirty-four at Drury Lane, thirty-one at Lincoln's Inn Fields, four at the Haymarket, five at Richmond, and one at Southwark Fair. Their attendance was greatest during the 1714-15 season, a time when the family was at pains to be introduced to its new subjects — 30 nights at Drury Lane, twenty-nine of opera at the King's Theatre, and one at the newly-opened Lincoln's Inn Fields. It was lowest in the 1724-25 season, with only four command performances. During the Jacobite Rebellion (September 1715) the royals still managed fifteen nights at the playhouse; during the débacle known as the South Sea Bubble (September 1720) they appeared only fourteen times. But in the thirteen seasons of the reign the Royal Family and its followers established the public taste as follows: one hundred and forty-one nights of comedy, twenty-eight nights of tragedy, one hundred and thirty nights at the opera. They were present at twelve nights of Shakespeare's history plays and eighty-three nights of farce and entertainments. While they enjoyed some nineteen plays from the early 17th century, they much preferred some sixty-seven Restoration plays, together with thirty-odd new plays and operas. Whatever the verdict as to George I as King, he and the House of Hanover began a continuing public support for the London theatres of the eighteenth century.

GENEALOGICAL TABLE 2

Children of King George II and Queen Caroline

GEORGE AUGUSTUS, 1683-1760; reigned as King George II 1727-1760;
married (1705) Caroline of Anspach (1683-1737)

Their Children

1. FREDERICK LEWIS (often spelt LOUIS), 1707-1751
   Prince of Wales 1727-1751
   m. Augusta of Saxe-Gotha
   [their son reigned as King George III 1760-1820]

2. ANNE, 1709-1759, Princess Royal
   m. William IV, Prince of Orange

3. AMELIA, 1711-1786

4. CAROLINE, 1713-1757

5. GEORGE WILLIAM, 1717-1718

6. WILLIAM AUGUSTUS, 1721-1765
   Duke of Cumberland 1726-1765

7. MARY, 1723-1772
   m. Frederick, Landgrave of Hesse-Cassel

8. LOUISA, 1724-1751
   m. Frederick V, King of Denmark

Chapter II

THE REIGN OF GEORGE II, 1727-60

On 14 June 1727 George Augustus was told of the death of his father at Osnabrück, Germany. As Prince of Wales he had commanded performances in the London theatres and was present at forty-three more to a total of one hundred and eighty-three nights. He was 44 years old at his accession to the throne as George II and reigned for another thirty-three years. While his subjects, familiar with his hatred of his father, expected him to reverse all that George I had done, the new King actually grew more and more like his father. His new court was anything but lively, and George and Caroline adopted a new policy of economy, together with a mania for strict observance of court etiquette and absolute punctuality. But his love of things theatrical was not abated. According to details in *The London Stage Pts. 2, 3 and 4,* George II, despite his new responsibilities in government, commanded one hundred and three performances and was present at one hundred and fifty-seven more before his death in 1760; and if we were to add the performances at Hampton Court ordered by the King, the total would be greater. Unfortunately we find record of only one night, that of 18 October 1731, when the Drury Lane company acted Farquhar's *The Recruiting Officer* followed by dancing.[1] The *Daily Advertiser* for 17 June 1731 had commented: 'His Majesty's Servants of Drury Lane are getting everything in Readiness to act at Hampton-Court twice a week...and we hear they are to Act there the first time on Monday next.' But as late as 9 July 1731 the *Daily Journal* had this to announce: 'We hear that a Playhouse is to be erected on Hampton-Green, with all Expedition, for acting of Plays for the Entertainment of the Royal Family.' The latter announcement would appear the more probable, since the only recorded performance was not given until Monday, 18 October.

One hundred and forty-four of George II's evenings were devoted to fifty-two operas and four oratorios at the King's Theatre, at Covent Garden, and at the Little Theatre in the Haymarket. His favourites were: *Porus* (Metastasio-Humphreys-Handel, 1731), eleven nights; *Alexander* (Rolli-Handel, 1726), *Siroe* (Metastasio-Haym-Handel, 1728), *Ariadne (in Creta)* (Colman-Handel, 1734), seven nights each; *Sosarmes* (Noris-Humphreys-Handel, 1732), six nights; *Orlando* (Bracciuoli-Humphreys-Handel, 1733), *Admetus* (Aureli-Handel, 1727), five nights each.

Some operas and musical evenings he heard but once were: *Richard the First, Lotharius, Julius Caesar, Floridante, Parnasso in Festa, The Feast of Alexander, The Feast of Hymen, Atalanta, Berenice, Orestes, Sabrina,* and *Alcina,* the compositions of Handel, Rolli, Porpora, Haym, Purcell-Clarke-Leveridge, and two pasticcio productions. Once again Handel is represented by seven of the operas, and by three further musical entertainments - *Parnasso in Festa* at the King's Theatre (23 March 1734) in celebration of the marriage of Anne, Princess Royal, to the Prince of Orange; *The Feast of Alexander,* (25 February 1736) at Covent Garden; and *Atalanta* (12 May 1736) at Covent Garden, in honour of the royal nuptials of Frederick Lewis, Prince of Wales, and Princess Augusta of Saxe-Gotha.

One hundred and twelve of George II's evenings were given to stage plays at Drury Lane, Lincoln's Inn Fields, Covent Garden, the Haymarket, and Hampton Court. During his reign George II chose comedies on seventy-two occasions, twenty-two nights of tragedy, twenty-six nights of Shakespeare, and forty-four nights of afterpieces (including thirty-three pantomimes). His favourite playwrights were: Shakespeare (twenty-six times); Vanbrugh (twelve times); Colley Cibber (ten times); Farquhar, Dryden, and Mrs. Centlivre (six times each); Davenant, Congreve, Jonson (four times each); Rowe, Otway, Buckingham, Garrick (three times each); Etherege, Ravenscroft, Mrs. Behn, Fielding, Fletcher, Steele, Shadwell, Hoadly, and Tate (twice each). Five nights were devoted to musical entertainment.

Among his favourite stage plays we find: *Henry IV, Part 1,* eight nights; *Henry VIII, The False Friend, The Provok'd Wife, The Busy Body, The Refusal, The Suspicious Husband,* three nights each; *The Relapse, The Stratagem, The Provok'd Husband, The Alchymist, Richard III, The London Cuckolds, Macbeth, The Fatal Marriage, The Tempest, The Recruiting Officer, The Double Dealer, Venice Preserv'd, The Rehearsal, The Fair Quaker of Deal, A Bold Stroke for a Wife, Othello, Hamlet,* and *Every Man in His Humour,* two performances each. Of the forty-three afterpieces he preferred *The Necromancer,* four nights, and *Apollo and Daphne* and *Perseus and Andromeda,* two nights each.

George II commanded sixteen benefit nights, ten at Drury Lane, four at Covent Garden, and two at Lincoln's Inn Fields. Mrs. Porter was the actress most honoured, with eight nights of royal patronage (seven at Drury Lane and one at Covent Garden), followed by her colleague Mrs. Oldfield at Drury Lane and Signora Barberini, dancer at Covent Garden, two benefits. Mrs. Younger and Francisque at Lincoln's Inn Fields, Mlle. Sallé at Covent Garden, and Ann Auretti at Drury Lane, each enjoyed a command benefit. Unfortunately for the acting profession, benefit nights by royal command were destined to be curtailed during George II's reign.

Seasons in which the King attended the greatest number of times were those of 1730-31 (thirty-four times), 1731-32 (thirty-four times), 1732-33 (thirty times), 1733-34 (twenty-four times), 1727-28 (sixteen times), 1734-35 and 1735-36 (fifteen times each), 1746-47 (ten times). Some explanation for such a varied schedule is to be found in contemporary court life.

The death of Queen Caroline in November 1737, after a long and painful ordeal, accounts for the King's absence from the playhouses during the season 1737-38. After two operas in 1736-37 (*Berenice* at Covent Garden, 18 May 1737, and *Sabrina* at the King's Theatre, 31 May 1737), the Queen's terminal illness kept the King from the public until the period of public mourning was ended, when he first attended Covent Garden on the evening of 11 January 1739 to see *King Henry the Fifth* and the pantomime *The Royal Chace.* On 22 January he again visited Covent Garden for *Macbeth* and *Perseus and Andromeda.*

The very light or blank seasons of 1741-42 to 1745-46 found the King occupied with governmental difficulties after the fall of the Walpole administration in 1742, and with wars at home and abroad - first the war with Spain and later France, which broke out in September 1739, and then the appearance of the Young Pretender in the summer of 1745. Presumably there was little time or occasion for theatrical attendance during this period, despite the arrival on the stage of David Garrick (who commenced at Drury Lane in 1742), and despite the fact that the King's victory against the French at Dettingen in 1743 had increased his popularity. However, with the collapse of the Jacobite rebellion and a strengthened political ministry in 1746, the King made ten appearances at the theatres in the season 1746-47.

While George II continued to favour some Elizabethan plays and those of the Restoration, he showed a growing interest in those of his own generation. Among contemporary plays he chose *The Provok'd Husband* (1728), *The London Merchant* (1731), *Orestes* (1731), *the Modern Husband* (1732), *The Miser* (1733), *The Intriguing Chambermaid* (1734), *Arlequin Astrologue* (1735), *Miss In Her Teens* (1747), *The Suspicious Husband* (1747), and modern adaptations of such older pieces as *The Rehearsal* (1742), *Every Man in His Humour* (1751), *The Chances* (1754), and *Romeo and Juliet* (1748).

The new King was destined to repeat the unhappy relationship between himself and his son, Frederick Lewis, Prince of Wales, that had existed toward his father in the previous reign. 'Poor Fred', born in Hanover in 1706, was 21 at his father's accession and hated by both his parents from birth. George Augustus perceived his oldest son as a 'half-witted coxcomb' who would inevitably become the leader of opposition to his government. He determined to reduce Frederick's social influence by keeping the young man on a reduced allowance, until the Prince's marriage to Princess Augusta of Saxe-Gotha in 1736 necessitated a separate home and an increased income.

GENEALOGICAL TABLE 3

Children of Frederick and Augusta, Prince and Princess of Wales

FREDERICK LEWIS (often spelt LOUIS), 1707-1751; Prince of Wales 1729-1751; married (1736) Augusta of Saxe-Gotha (1719-1772)

Their Children

1. AUGUSTA, 1737-1813
   m. Charles, Duke of Brunswick-Wolfenbüttel

2. GEORGE WILLIAM FREDERICK, 1738-1820
   Prince of Wales 1751-1760
   m. Charlotte of Mecklenburg-Strelitz
   reigned as King George III 1760-1820

3. EDWARD AUGUSTUS, 1739-1767, Duke of York and Albany

4. ELIZABETH CAROLINE, 1741-1759

5. WILLIAM HENRY, 1743-1805, Duke of Gloucester and Edinburgh
   m. Maria Walpole, Dowager Countess of Waldegrave

6. HENRY FREDERICK, 1745-1790, Duke of Cumberland 1765-1790
   m. Anne Horton (Luttrell)

7. LOUISA ANNE, 1749-1768

8. FREDERICK WILLIAM, 1750-1765

9. CAROLINE MATILDA, 1751-1775
   m. Christian VII, King of Denmark

Frederick Lewis was to develop attendance at the public theatres as a cultural and political enterprise. As the bachelor Prince of Wales he attended two hundred and sixty-four nights, one hundred of these 'By Command'; and after his marriage in 1736 he and his Princess commanded two hundred and thirty-six nights and were present on twenty more occasions. At his residence in Pall Mall Frederick liked to appear as the sponsor of new operas, holding rehearsals as gala entertainment for his guests. On 25 December 1733 the *Daily Post* reported: 'Last Night there was a Rehearsal of a new Opera at the Prince of Wales's House in the Royal Gardens in Pall-Mall, where was present a great Concourse of the Nobility and Quality of both Sexes; some of the Choicest Voices and Hands assisted in the Performance.'[2] Again in 1734 the *London Daily Post and General Advertiser* for 30 November reported: 'Last Night there was a Rehearsal of a new Opera before his Royal Highness the Prince of Wales at his House in Pall-Mall, in which Farinelli and Senesino each of them perform'd a Part.'[3] The same newspaper for 17 March 1737 remarked of *Alexander's Feast* at Covent Garden the previous evening: 'The Prince and Princess of Wales seem'd to be highly entertain'd, insomuch that his Royal Highness commanded Mr.Handel's Concerto on the Organ to be repeated.'[4]

In politics the Prince was quite openly opposed to Sir Robert Walpole and his government. The *Daily Advertiser* for 30 March 1736 remarked that: 'We hear that his Royal Highness the Prince of Wales honour'd *Pasquin* [at the Haymarket Theatre] last Night with his Presence, when it was acted the twentieth Time to a crowded Audience...and many thousands of People turn'd away for want of room.'[5] This was followed on 18 April 1737 with another evening at the Haymarket for Fielding's *The Historical Register* and *Eurydice Hiss'd,* about which the *Egmont Diary* tells us: 'To the Haymarket Playhouse, where a farce was acted called Eurydice First [=Hiss'd], an allegory on the loss of the Excise Bill. The whole was a satire on Sir Robert Walpole, and I observed that when any strong passages fell, the Prince, who was there, clapped, especially when in favour of liberty.'[6] Evidently

Frederick Lewis was a specialist in public relations; we read in the *General Advertiser* for 14 March 1744: 'Last Night their Royal Highnesses the Prince and Princess of Wales were at the Theatre Royal in Covent Garden to see the Merchant of Venice; when the Song of *Britons strike home* was commanded to be sung, which was accordingly done, with the Chorus's, accompanied by Trumpets, Kettledrums, etc., and met with the Greatest Applause.'[7]

In the many celebrations of the marriage of Frederick Lewis and Augusta, theatres vied with each other to salute the royal couple, especially Covent Garden. When the Prince and Princess attended a command performance of *King Henry the Eighth* and the pantomime *The Fall of Phaeton* on 5 May 1736 at Drury Lane, the *Daily Post and General Advertiser* described the night in its edition of 6 May as follows: 'There was an exceeding great Audience, and great Numbers of Quality both in the Boxes and Pit. Their Highnesses' Box was handsomely ornamented....'[8] Seven days later, on 12 May, Covent Garden presented a spectacular piece called *Atalanta: In Honour of the Royal Nuptials of their Royal Highnesses the Prince and Princess of Wales.* The next day the *Daily Post and General Advertiser* reported the production in great detail: 'Last Night was perform'd... Atalanta...in which was a new Set of Scenes painted in Honour to this Happy Union.... There were present their Majesties, the Duke, and the Four Princesses.'[9]

All these preparations - and their Royal Highnesses not present? It is plain to see that the family feud was continuing when we note that the Prince and Princess of Wales attended Drury Lane that evening for a performance of Addison's *Cato* with dancing. Covent Garden did not give up hope, however, for as late as 6 November *Alcina* was sung at Covent Garden by command of the royal couple.[10]

Before his marriage, Frederick as Prince of Wales commanded nights for twenty-four benefit performances - ten at Drury Lane, ten at Lincoln's Inn Fields, three at Covent Garden, and one at the Haymarket. Mrs. Younger (four nights) and Miss Holliday (four nights) were the Prince's favourites at Lincoln's Inn Fields, with Mlle. Sallé (two nights), and Quin, Mrs. Bullock, and

Theobald with one night each. At Drury Lane the honoured included: Desnoyer (three nights); Mrs. Cibber (two nights); Cibber, Jr. and Mrs. Cibber, Bowman and Mrs. Walter, Mrs. Booth, and Mrs. Heron (one night each). Mrs. Younger was given one night at Covent Garden, and John Dennis one at the Haymarket. After their marriage the royal couple commanded on fifty evenings - thirty-three benefits at Drury Lane, seventeen at Covent Garden. James Quin was honoured on six evenings; Desnoyer on five; Mrs. Clive, four; Mrs. Porter, Garrick, and Beard three each; Lalauze, Salway, Mrs. Woffington, Mrs. Cibber, two nights each. Actors honoured on only one benefit occasion included: Miss Holliday, Giffard, Milward, Mills, Mrs. Mills, Wright, Mlle. Chateauneuf, Chaman, Essex, Fausson, Macklin, Picq, Signora Domitilla, Dubuisson, Mlle. Bonneval, Ann Auretti, Barry, Pritchard (Treasurer), and Cervetto (violin-cello).

Frederick Lewis heard a total of forty-seven operas and eight oratorios in his brief lifetime, and many of these became his favourites: *The Beggar's Opera* (Gay-Pepusch, 1728), thirteen nights; *Porus* (Metastasio-Humphreys, 1731), nine nights; *Macbeth* (Locke-Johnson-Leveridge, 1702), seven nights; *Alexander* (Rolli-Handel, 1726), five nights; *Sosarmes* (Noris-Humphreys-Handel, 1732), *Rinaldo* (Hill-Handel, 1711), *Ariadne (in Creta)* (Colman-Handel, 1734), *Parthenope* (Stampiglia-Handel, 1730), *Admetus* (Aureli-Handel, 1727), *Aetius* (Metastasio-Humphreys-Handel, 1733), *Esther* (Humphreys-Handel, 1732), *Acis and Galatea* (Gay-Handel, 1731) and *Orlando* (Bracciuoli-Humphreys-Handel, 1733), four nights each; *Deborah* (Humphreys-Handel, 1733), *Otho* (Haym-Handel, 1723), *Artaxerxes* (Metastasio-Hasse-Broschi, 1734), *Alcina* (Marchi-Handel, 1735), *Alexander's Feast* (Dryden-Handel, 1737), *Rodelinda* (Salvi-Haym-Handel, 1725), three nights each; *Cato* (Metastasio-Humphreys, 1732), *Ptolemy* (Haym-Handel, 1728), *Griselda* (Zeno-Rolli-Buononcini, 1722), *Semiramis* (Roy-Destouches, 1718), *Pastor Fido* (Rossi-Handel, 1712), *Polifemo* (Rolli-Porpora, 1735), *Adriano* (Metastasio-Veracini, 1735), and *Orpheus* (Rolli-Pasticcio, 1736), two nights each.

As for stage productions, the Prince of Wales witnessed one hundred and twenty-six mainpieces, attending one evening at Hampton Court; eight at Richmond; one at Reynolds' Booth, Bartholomew Fair; forty-two at Lincoln's Inn Fields; sixteen at the Haymarket; one hundred and twenty-six at Covent Garden; and two hundred and twenty-four at Drury Lane. Of these eighty-five were comedies, thirty-five were tragedies, with six history plays of Shakespeare. His favourite dramas were *Cato* (thirteen nights), *The Recruiting Officer* (twelve nights), *Henry VIII* and *The Busy Body,* eleven nights each. Among the seventy-seven afterpieces which had come into vogue he preferred *The Devil to Pay* (nineteen nights), *Perseus and Andromeda* (fifteen nights), *Apollo and Daphne* (thirteen nights), and *The Lottery* (twelve nights).

At the sudden death of the Prince of Wales on 19 March 1751 his widow Augusta became the Dowager Princess of Wales, and his eldest son, George William Frederick, became Prince of Wales at the age of twelve. His mother observed a suitable period of mourning, and it was not until the season of 1753-54 that she was to grace public theatrical performances once more. Her first appearance, according to Richard Cross, Drury Lane prompter, was at Covent Garden Theatre when she commanded a performance of *The Siege of Damascus* with *Harlequin Sorcerer* on 3 January 1754. She was to command six performances - four at Covent Garden and two at Drury Lane - and attend nine other nights before her death on 8 February 1772. This occurred in the next reign but it is convenient to note it here.

George William Frederick was taken to the theatre at an early age. Prior to his father's death in 1751 he had experienced twenty-six nights of varied entertainments - twenty-three at Covent Garden, two at Drury Lane, and one at the Haymarket. Of these nights, eleven were plays of Shakespeare - *Henry VIII,* five nights; *Henry IV, Part 1,* two nights; *The Merry Wives of Windsor,* two nights; *Othello* and *Hamlet,* one night each. The other evenings were devoted to *Cato* and *The Rehearsal,* two nights each; *The Beggar's Opera,* two nights; and *Aesop, The Fair Penitent, Lady Jane*

Grey, A Duke and No Duke, Mariamne, The Distrest Mother, All for Love, Arlequin Triumphante, The Double Falsehood, one night each. Of twelve nights of afterpieces he favoured *The Rape of Proserpine, Apollo and Daphne, Perseus and Andromeda,* and *Damon and Phillida,* two nights each. It is interesting to speculate on how such a repertoire influenced the growing boy and how much was due to the social amenities of his semi-public life.

Anne, Princess Royal, attended public entertainment on one hundred and forty-five nights prior to her marriage to William IV, Prince of Orange, on 14 March 1734. The Prince arrived in London on 8 November 1733 amid illuminations and bonfires in the city. He and Anne graced the theatre and opera scene thirteen times after the wedding. The last performance they witnessed was at the Haymarket Theatre on 1 November 1734, where they saw *L'Avare* and *Le Réunion des Amours.* In honour of the royal wedding Handel was represented at the King's Theatre by his Serenata *Parnasso in Festa* which the newly-weds heard on three occasions.

Among some forty mainpieces that the Princess favoured were: *Henry VIII* and *The Careless Husband,* three nights each; *The Provok'd Husband, The Provok'd Wife, Henry IV, Part 1, Themistocles, Lover of His Country, Love Makes a Man,* and *The Amorous Widow,* two nights each. Her favourite afterpieces were: *Perseus and Andromeda,* three nights; *Damon and Phillida, Cephalus and Procris, Apollo and Daphne, The Devil to Pay,* and *The Country Revels,* two nights each.

As Princess Royal she attended opera on ninety-four nights and preferred the following: *Porus,* thirteen nights; *Alexander, Ariadne (in Creta),* seven nights each; *Rinaldo, Rodelinda, Siroe, Aetius, Sosarmes, Deborah,* and *Griselda,* four nights each; *Otho, Ptolemy, Admetus, Arbaces, Parnasso in Festa, Julius Caesar, Parthenope,* three nights each; *Wenceslaus, Tamerlane, Coriolanus, Cato, Acis and Galatea,* and *Semiramis,* two nights each.

The two spinster daughters of George II and Queen Caroline were Princess Amelia (born in 1711) and Princess Caroline (born in 1713). They had been introduced along with the Princess

Royal to the theatres and opera by their grandfather. Princess Amelia attended on two hundred and fifty-eight nights (thirty-seven command performances, two hundred and twenty-one other occasions), and Princess Caroline on two hundred and fifty nights (sixty-five command performances, one hundred and eighty-five other occasions). They often appeared together at the opera. Among the forty-five operas and oratorios they heard, Amelia's preferences were: *Porus,* nine nights; *Ariadne (in Creta),* eight nights; *Rinaldo, Siroe, Orlando,* five nights each; *Otho, Aetius, Alexander, Griselda,* and *Deborah,* four nights each; *Scipio, Admetus, Arbaces, Alcina,* three nights each; *Rodelinda, Julius Caesar, Ormisda, Parthenope, Tamerlane, Coriolanus, Cato, Artaxerxes,* two nights each. Princess Caroline heard the same operas and oratorios, but her attendance varied by one or more nights.

Together they witnessed over eighty mainpieces and favoured: *The Stratagem,* seven nights; *The Provok'd Wife* and *Richard III,* six nights each; *The Provok'd Husband, The Double Gallant* and *Love Makes a Man,* four nights each; *The Spanish Fryar, The Conscious Lovers, Hamlet, The Man of Mode, Arlequin Astrologue, The Merchant of Venice,* and *The Rehearsal,* three nights each; *Love's Last Shift, The Constant Couple, Henry VIII, The Merry Wives of Windsor, Henry IV, Part 1* and *Part 2, The Busy Body, The Tender Husband, Venice Preserv'd, The Amorous Widow, Wit Without Money, The Way of the World, Arlequin Balourd,* and *The Committee,* two nights each. Princess Caroline enjoyed afterpieces more than her sister, forty-two in all. Her favourites were: *Apollo and Daphne,* six nights; *Perseus and Andromeda,* five nights; *Harlequin a Sorcerer, Harlequin Doctor Faustus, Harlequin Hulla, Harlequin Restor'd, The Royal Chase, The Dragon of Wantley, Harlequin Always Harlequin, Harlequin Grand Volgi, Columbine Courtesan, Harlequin Shipwreck'd, The Country Revels,* and *The Mock Doctor,* two nights each. Princess Amelia saw almost the same number of afterpieces but favoured only nine: *Perseus and Andromeda,* six nights; *Apollo and Daphne,* four nights; *Harlequin Doctor Faustus* and *The Dragon of Wantley,* three nights each; *Cephalus and Procris, The Country Revels, Arlequin Hulla, Harlequin Always Harlequin,* and *Harlequin Shipwreck'd,* two nights each.

The two youngest daughters of George II and Caroline were Mary and Louisa. Princess Mary married Frederick, Landgrave of Hesse-Cassel, in 1740. Prior to her wedding she had attended ninety performances. In the season 1746-47 she returned from Germany for a visit and attended Covent Garden for two performances - *Richard III* on 31 October 1746 and *Hamlet* with *The King and the Miller of Mansfield* on 10 November 1746. Princess Louisa married Frederick V of Denmark in 1743. Prior to her marriage she had attended one hundred and twenty-two performances, nine of them 'By Command'.

Edward Augustus, Duke of York and Albany was the second son of Frederick Lewis and Augusta, and grandson of George II. During his grandfather's reign he witnessed forty-eight performances: twenty-seven at Covent Garden, nineteen at Drury Lane, one at the Haymarket Theatre and one at Marylebone. His favourite plays were: *Henry VIII,* four nights; *Mariamne, Henry IV, Part 1, Cato, The Merry Wives of Windsor, Romeo and Juliet, Every Man in His Humour,* and *The Beggar's Opera,* two nights each. Among the afterpieces he preferred *The Rape of Proserpine, Apollo and Daphne, Perseus and Andromeda, The Chaplet, Catherine and Petruchio,* and *The Knights.*

His brother, William Henry, Duke of Gloucester and Edinburgh, attended on twenty-seven nights at Drury Lane (fourteen performances) and Covent Garden (thirteen performances). His favourite mainpieces were: *Henry VIII, Henry IV, Part 1, The Beggar's Opera,* and *Romeo and Juliet,* two nights each. Among the afterpieces he preferred only *The Chaplet* on two occasions.

Another grandson of George II was Henry Frederick, Duke of Cumberland and Strathearn, who was not an avid theatregoer. He did, however, manage to attend seventeen performances during his father's lifetime. The last grandson of George II, Frederick William, was only 15 years old at his death in 1765, but he had attended the theatre during his grandfather's reign, going to eight performances at Drury Lane and four at Covent Garden.

The four daughters of Frederick Lewis, and grand-daughters of George II, were Augusta, Elizabeth Caroline, Louisa Ann, and Caroline Matilda. The Princesses Elizabeth Caroline and Louisa Ann were to die in their teens, while Princess Augusta married Charles, Duke of Brunswick-Wolfenbüttel, and Princess Caroline Matilda became the bride of Christian VII, King of Denmark.

Princess Augusta witnessed forty-nine performances during her grandfather's reign, thirty at Covent Garden, eighteen at Drury Lane, and one at the Haymarket Theatre. Her favourite mainpiece was *Henry VIII*, which she enjoyed on five evenings. Others were *The Beggar's Opera, Henry IV, Part 1, A Duke and No Duke, The Rehearsal, Mariamne, Cato, The Merry Wives of Windsor, Every Man in His Humour*, two nights each; *Henry V, Comus*, and *The Jovial Crew*, one night each. Among the afterpieces she preferred *Perseus and Andromeda, Apollo and Daphne*, three nights each; *Fortunatus, Catherine and Petruchio*, two nights each; *The Rape of Proserpine, The Chaplet*, and *The Knights*, one night each. Princess Elizabeth Caroline attended twenty-five performances at the public theatres, thirteen at Covent Garden and twelve at Drury Lane. The Princess died on 4 September 1759. The two youngest sisters, Louisa Ann and Caroline Matilda, attended on only one evening during this reign at Covent Garden (26 April 1760) for the performance of *The Jovial Crew* and *The Knights*.

SUMMARY OF ATTENDANCE, 1727-60

The reign of George II was terminated by his sudden death on 25 October 1760. During the thirty-three years since his accession to the throne the record in *The London Stage Parts 2, 3, and 4* shows that a member, several members, or the entire Royal Family supported the theatre and opera to the amazing total of two thousand one hundred and thirty-eight appearances - eight hundred and seventeen at Drury Lane, five hundred and sixty-five at the King's Theatre, five hundred at Covent Garden, one hundred and eleven at Lincoln's Inn Fields, eighty-five at the Haymarket, eighteen at Richmond, seven at Hampton Court, and thirteen at the fair booths of Bartholomew Fair and

Tottenham Court. The family's attendance was greatest in the early 1730's: e.g. 1731-32 - thirty-two nights at the King's Theatre, twenty-two at Drury Lane, seven at Lincoln's Inn Fields, two at St.James Palace, and one each at Hampton Court, Richmond, and Tottenham Court, sixty-six performances in all; and 1734-35 - twenty-nine at the Haymarket, fifteen at Drury Lane, twelve at Covent Garden, seven at the King's Theatre, three at Richmond, and one each at Lincoln's Inn Fields, Goodman's Fields, and the Haymarket, sixty-nine nights in all. Family attendance was lowest in the season 1745-46, when only three nights were devoted to the theatre (two at Covent Garden and one at Drury Lane), until the invasion by the Young Pretender was defeated by the Duke of Cumberland.

THE ROYAL FAMILY AT THE THEATRES AND OPERA, 1727-60

	DL	CG	K'S	HAY	LIF	HC	RI	FAIRS, etc
George II and Queen Caroline	74	49	125	2	9	1	0	0
Frederick Lewis and Augusta, Prince and Princess of Wales	230	130	88	18	50	1	8	3
Augusta, Dowager Princess of Wales	4	11	0	0	0	0	0	0
George William Frederick, Prince of Wales from 1751	47	54	0	1	0	0	0	0
William Augustus, Duke of Cumberland	89	43	23	11	7	1	1	2
Anne, Princess Royal	39	2	99	3	10	1	2	1
Princess Amelia	88	46	94	12	13	1	2	1
Princess Caroline	87	37	91	14	17	0	3	1
Princess Mary	25	25	23	11	2	1	1	2
Princess Louisa	51	30	22	11	3	1	1	2
Edward Augustus, Duke of York	19	27	0	1	0	0	0	1
William Henry, Duke of Gloucester	14	13	0	0	0	0	0	0
Henry Frederick, Duke of Cumberland	12	6	0	0	0	0	0	0

	DL	CG	K'S	HAY	LIF	HC	RI	FAIRS, etc
Prince Frederick William	8	4	0	0	0	0	0	0
Princess Augusta	18	30	0	1	0	0	0	0
Princess Elizabeth Caroline	12	13	0	0	0	0	0	0
Princess Louisa Ann	0	1	0	0	0	0	0	0
Princess Caroline Matilda	0	1	0	0	0	0	0	0
Total	817	522	565	85	111	7	18	13

It is well to note that the attendance pattern for the Royal Family and its followers differs from that of the previous reign only in the number of performances they witnessed, not in their preferences. The pleasure of the royal family as a whole largely insisted on comedy, farce, opera and musical entertainment as opposed to tragedy and the history plays of Shakespeare and other playwrights. Special delight was in the afterpieces, farce, ballad opera and pantomimes (the more spectacular the better), since the regular appearance of these forms set the course for the repertoire that was to persist in dominating the theatre into the next century and beyond. It would appear that the royals continued to establish public taste as noted in the following chart.

TYPES OF ENTERTAINMENT ON ROYAL ATTENDANCE NIGHTS, 1727-60

	C	T	F	HP	OP	BO	OR	PA/ENT
George II and Queen Caroline	72	22	7	12	132	3	10	37
Frederick Lewis and Augusta, Prince and Princess of Wales	230	97	39	33	96	100	14	127
Augusta, Dowager Princess of Wales	4	6	4	2	1	1	0	5
George William Frederick, Prince of Wales from 1751	27	47	14	11	1	10	1	28
William Augustus, Duke of Cumberland	76	19	24	7	30	12	2	36
Anne, Princess Royal	32	11	6	7	94	10	5	14
Princess Amelia	84	29	20	12	105	14	8	35
Princess Caroline	85	30	23	11	99	12	6	48

	C	T	F	HP	OP	BO	OR	PA/ENT
Princess Mary	33	10	21	5	29	3	0	36
Princess Louisa	52	16	24	8	26	4	1	35
Edward Augustus, Duke of York	11	21	7	7	1	4	0	14
William Henry, Duke of Gloucester	5	14	3	3	1	2	0	9
Henry Frederick, Duke of Cumberland	5	9	3	0	0	5	0	8
Prince Frederick William	4	5	5	2	1	0	0	2
Princess Augusta	13	19	8	8	1	4	0	16
Princess Elizabeth Caroline	5	11	3	4	1	1	0	9
Princess Louisa Ann	0	0	1	0	0	1	0	0
Princess Caroline Matilda	0	0	1	0	0	1	0	0
Total	738	366	213	132	618	187	47	459

While they witnessed sixty-seven nights of plays that had been written during the sixteenth and early seventeenth centuries (probably attending as a matter of custom and duty), nearly all members of the royal family seemed to prefer the post-Restoration plays of the later seventeenth century (four hundred and thirty-three nights) and plays from the contemporary eighteenth-century repertoire (over one thousand six hundred nights). Such was the taste-pattern for theatre and opera established during the reign of George II. It was extended during the following reign of George III.

GENEALOGICAL TABLE 4

Children of King George III and Queen Charlotte

GEORGE WILLIAM FREDERICK, 1738-1820; reigned as King George
III 1760-1820;
married (1761) Charlotte Sophia of Mecklenburg-Strelitz (1744-1818).

Their Children

1. GEORGE AUGUSTUS FREDERICK, 1762-1830
    Prince of Wales 1762-1820
    m. Caroline of Brunswick; 1 daughter, Charlotte, 1796-1817;
    reigned as King George IV 1820-1830

2. FREDERICK, 1763-1827, Duke of York and Albany 1767-1827
    m. Frederika of Prussia

3. WILLIAM, 1765-1837, Duke of Clarence
    m. Adelaide of Saxe-Meiningen; 2 daughters, died in infancy;
    reigned as King William IV 1830-1837

4. CHARLOTTE, 1766-1828, Princess Royal
    m. Frederick I, King of Würtemburg

5. EDWARD, 1767-1820, Duke of Kent
    m. Victoria of Saxe-Coburg-Saalfield
    [their daughter reigned as Queen Victoria 1837-1901]

6. AUGUSTA, 1768-1840

7. ELIZABETH, 1770-1840
    m. Frederick, Landgrave of Hesse-Homburg

8. ERNEST AUGUSTUS 1771-1851, Duke of Cumberland 1799-1851
    m. Frederika of Mecklenburg-Strelitz; line continued as sovereigns of
    Hanover; as King Ernst August reigned as King of Hanover 1837-1851

9. AUGUSTUS FREDERICK, 1773-1843, Duke of Sussex
    m. (1) Augusta Murray; (2) Cecilia Underwood

10. ADOLPHUS FREDERICK, 1774-1850, Duke of Cambridge
    m. Augusta of Hesse-Cassel

11. MARY, 1776-1857
    m. William Frederick, 1776-1834, Duke of Gloucester and Edinburgh 1805-1834

12. SOPHIA, 1777-1848

13. OCTAVIUS, 1779-1783

14. ALFRED, 1780-1782

15. AMELIA, 1783-1810

Chapter III

THE REIGN OF GEORGE III, 1760-1820

George William Frederick (b.1738) was the first sovereign since Queen Anne whose native language was English and spoken without a Germanic accent. Under the supervision of his mother, Augusta, Princess of Wales, and her close friend the Earl of Bute, George's education was as thorough as possible for a young man not outstanding in academic studies. In the preceding chapter we have already seen how such education included visits to the London theatres, especially Covent Garden, beginning when he was only six years old. In the autumn of 1748, at the age of ten, he was taken, with Prince Edward and Princess Augusta, to see James Quin's performance of Addison's *Cato* at Covent Garden on 25 October. A second performance of this tragedy on 21 December was witnessed by the three children and their younger sister the Princess Elizabeth Caroline. All this appears to have been in preparation for their appearance in a private production of *Cato* by the royal children at Leicester House directed by none other than James Quin. This venture has been described by the author of *George III, His Court and Family* (1820):

> To accustom the young Princes to oratory, private theatricals had been some time in preparation at Leicester House, and the tragedy of Cato was got ready for rehearsal on the last day of 1748. The final representation took place on the 4th of January, 1749, when as many of the young Princes and Princesses as were old enough, together with several youths of quality, made their debut before a numerous assembly of rank and fashion, and were received with great applause.

DRAMATIS PERSONAE

Portius .... Prince George.
Juba .... Prince Edward.
Cato .... Master Nugent.
Sempronius .... Master Evelyn.
Lucius .... Master Montague.
Decius .... Lord Millington.
Syphax .... Lord North's Son.
Marcus .... Master Madden.
Marcia .... Princess Augusta.
Lucia .... Princess Elizabeth.

The Prologue was recited by Prince George:-

To speak with freedom, dignity, and ease,
To learn those arts, which may hereafter please,
Wise authors say - let youth in earliest age,
Rehearse the poet's labours on the stage.

....

The epilogue was spoken by the Princess Augusta and Prince Edward alternately....[1]

Such experience was to stimulate the future King's delight in entertainments at the theatres and to set a custom in his public relations with his subjects. Jesse wrote: 'So frequent were his visits to the theatre, that the people of London are said to have been as well acquainted with his features as with those of their next-door neighbour. His glee during the performance of a broad farce, or at a droll hit in a pantomime, may at times have been somewhat too exuberantly manifested, but his subjects did not love him the less that he showed himself completely at home in the midst of them. Neither did his sense of the ridiculous prevent his enjoying the higher beauties of the drama....'[2] (See frontispiece.) By the beginning of the twentieth century the portrait was enlarged by Beckles Willson:

In town the king rarely missed an evening at the opera. He had not only a good ear for melody, but a taste for the most classical compositions. 'His Majesty's partiality for Handel's music was generally spoken of,' says Michael Kelly in his *Reminiscences,* 'but I believe it was not universally known what an excellent and correct judge he was of its merits.' Almost equally fond was George of the drama. He was as great and discriminating a playgoer as his royal successor Edward VII, and, it may be added, as catholic in his tastes. No point of action or dialogue appeared to escape him, and the laughter and applause which proceeded from the royal box coincided with the responsiveness of the intellectual pit... .'[3]

According to the record in *The London Stage pts 4 and 5,* from his accession in 1760 to the year 1800 King George III devoted six hundred and ninety evenings to the theatres of Drury Lane (two hundred and sixty-two nights), Covent Garden (two hundred and ninety-nine nights), the King's Theatre (ninety-eight nights), the Haymarket (twenty-eight nights), and the Pantheon (three nights). Of these occasions, two hundred and six were spent hearing eighty-three operas and musical mainpieces. His favourites were: *Acis and Galatea* (Gay-Handel, 1731), twenty-four nights; *The Duenna* (Sheridan-Linley and others, 1775), twelve nights; *La Buona Figliuola* (Goldoni-Piccini, 1766), eleven nights; *Love in a Village* (Bickerstaffe-Arne, 1762), eight nights; *Artaxerxes* (Metastasio-Hasse-Broschi, 1762), seven nights; *Il Vaggitori Tornati* (Bottarelli-Guglielmi, 1768), six nights; *The Spanish Barber* (Colman-Arnold, 1777) and *The Padlock* (Bickerstaffe-Dibdin, 1768), five nights each; *Gli Schiavi Per Amore* (Polumba-Paisiello, 1787), *Ramah Droog* (Cobb-Mazzinghi-Reeve, 1798) and *Peeping Tom* (O'Keeffe-Arnold, 1784), four nights each; *The Beggar's Opera* (Gay-Pepusch, 1728), *the Jovial Crew* (Roome-Concanen-Yonge-Unknown, 1731), *Ezio* (Metastasio-Handel, pasticcio, 1764), *Trakebarne Grand Mogul* (pasticcio, 1766), *La Buona Figliuola Maritata* (Colman-Piccini, 1767), *Il Barone Di Torre Forte* (Piccini, 1781), and *Summer Amusement* (Andrew-Miles-Arnold and others, 1779), three nights each.

One hundred and thirty evenings were devoted to oratorios. The King's favourites were the compositions of Handel: *Judas Maccabaeus* (Morell-Handel, 1748), twenty-three nights; *Messiah*

(Jennens-Handel, 1742), twenty-one nights; *Alexander's Feast* (Dryden-Handel, 1737), twenty nights; *Samson* (Hamilton-Handel, 1743), sixteen nights; *Dryden's Ode* (Dryden-Handel, 1739), ten nights; *L'Allegro, Il Penseroso ed Il Moderato* (Milton-Jennens-Handel, 1740), nine nights; *Israel in Egypt* (pasticcio, 1739) and *Deborah* (Humphreys-Handel, 1733), five nights each; and *Gideon* (Morell-Handel-pasticcio, 1764) three nights.

Three hundred and fifty-eight evenings were given to stage plays at Drury Lane, Covent Garden, and the Haymarket theatres. Of these, two hundred and ninety-seven pieces were comedies, thirty-two were tragedies, with twenty-six of the plays by Shakespeare. Four hundred and fifteen afterpieces have been recorded in the bills, including eighty-seven pantomimes. George III and his following may have been catholic in their tastes, as Beckles Willson would have it, but George's preferences were definitely on the side of comic entertainment.

The King's favourite stage plays included: *The Clandestine Marriage* (Garrick-Colman, 1766), twelve nights; *The Duenna* (Sheridan-Linley and others, 1775), eleven nights; *All in the Wrong* (Murphy, 1761), nine nights; *The Jealous Wife* (Colman, 1761) and *Rule a Wife and Have a Wife* (Fletcher-Garrick, 1756), eight nights each; *The Merchant of Venice* (Shakespeare), *Every Man in His Humour* (Jonson-Garrick, 1751), *The Belle's Stratagem* (Mrs. Cowley, 1780), *The Way to Keep Him* (Murphy, 1760), seven nights each; *Much Ado About Nothing* (Shakespeare), *A Bold Stroke for a Wife* (Mrs. Centlivre, 1718), *The Provok'd Husband* (C. Cibber-Vanbrugh, 1728), *The Chances* (Fletcher-Buckingham-Garrick, 1754), *The Rivals* (Sheridan, 1775), six nights each; *The Stratagem* (Farquhar, 1707), *As You Like It* (Shakespeare), *The Wonder* (Mrs. Centlivre, 1714), *The Busy Body* (Mrs. Centlivre, 1709), *The Miser* (Fielding, 1735), *The School for Scandal* (Sheridan, 1777), five nights each; *Jane Shore* (Rowe, 1714), *Measure for Measure* (Shakespeare), *The Merry Wives of Windsor* (Shakespeare), and *The Rehearsal* (Buckingham-Garrick, 1742), four nights each.

Seasons in which the King and Queen attended the greatest number of evenings were those of 1766-67 (forty times) and 1767-68 (thirty-three times). The least number of nights they were present occurred in the seasons of 1788-89 (once), 1795-96 (three times), 1789-90 (five times), and 1794-95 (seven times).

Immediately on his accession in 1760 the new king had invoked a programme of Shakespeare's history plays (see Annex, entry for 23 December 1760). As George III's reign progressed, however, his chief delight proved to be in the plays of his own age, particularly the works of Garrick, Colman, Murphy, Cumberland, and the adaptations of the ancients by Garrick and Colman.

King George III's four younger brothers fulfilled their public duties by attending the theatres mostly on family occasions. Otherwise their personal interests and activities took them elsewhere. His four sisters remained on the scene but a few years. Princess Augusta, the oldest, married Prince Charles of Brunswick-Wolfenbüttel; Princess Caroline Matilda, the youngest, was married by proxy at the age of 16 to King Christian VII of Denmark, was forced to endure imprisonment and ultimate exile in the castle of Zell, Hanover, and died at the age of 23 in May 1775. The middle two sisters were young maidens who died in their teens - Elizabeth Caroline in 1759 at 18 and Louisa Ann at 19 in 1768.

Concerning the children of George III and Charlotte, a brief word suffices.

John Clarke has characterized George Augustus Frederick, Prince of Wales and future King George IV, as an excellent conversationalist when he was moderately sober. 'He had a good memory and was an excellent mimic. George (Beau) Brummell said that he could have been the best comic actor in Europe. He was by far the most intelligent of the Hanoverians and could hold his own in the Sublime Society of Beefsteaks....'[4] While the prompters' official record of his theatre attendance is sketchy indeed, we know from Fanny Burney and other diarists of the age that the Prince was frequently observed entering just prior to the afterpiece of the evening and taking a place with friends and/or mistresses. His brothers fared just as poorly in the records. Perhaps the enthusiasm of the royal princes for public (if not private) attendance at the theatres was on the wane. The custom of the prompters is noting others than the sovereign as present was certainly being neglected. There is evidence from other sources that, at command performances at least, the king and queen would be accompanied by a clutch of daughters: the report of the assassination attempt (Annex, entry for 15 May 1800) shows that four princesses went with the monarchs on that occasion and that one royal duke, if no more, was in the audience independently.

The reign of George III was to continue for twenty more years beyond the scope of this survey, his death occurring on 29 January 1820. In 1810 his permanent insanity forbade any public appearance at the playhouses, but until that time he and the royal family had supported the theatres faithfully. By 15 May 1800 they are recorded as having appeared on seven hundred and fifty-five nights at the theatres in London - two hundred and seventy-three at Drury Lane, three hundred and fifty-two at Covent Garden, one hundred and two at the King's Theatre and the Pantheon, and twenty-eight at the Haymarket. The seasons in which the king and queen attended the greatest number of nights were those of: 1766-67 - seventeen at Covent Garden, twelve at the King's Theatre, eleven at Drury Lane, forty nights in all; 1767-68 - nineteen at Covent Garden, seven at Drury Lane, and seven at the King's Theatre, thirty-three nights in all; 1774-75 - thirteen at the King's Theatre, nine at Drury Lane, eight at Covent Garden, and five at the Haymarket, thirty-five nights in all.

Taking the royal family as a whole, and going by the available records which have to be considered incomplete, lowest attendances seem to have occurred in the seasons of 1788-89 (one night), 1789-90 (five nights), and 1795-96 (three nights). Reasons for a paucity of command performances, or official attendances by other members of the royal family, during the latter season might have included circumstances connected with the war in France, which had begun in 1793; during the first of these seasons the reason was probably the panic on the stock exchange in November 1788, coinciding with the king's illness which was itself a major bar to royal theatre-going while it lasted. In the autumn of 1788 the king was in poor health. We now recognise that he suffered from porphyria. By 5 November 1788, apparently lapsing into insanity, he had to be removed from Windsor Castle to his home in Kew until his recovery in March-April 1789. There was a full royal turn-out for the theatre on the one night attended during this season, 15 April at Covent Garden, despite, or perhaps because of, the Regency Bill crisis of February 1789, and the relief or alternatively chagrin consequent upon the king's improvement in health (which he signalled in March by dismissing all the Household officers who had supported the Prince of Wales's bid for power). This performance was commanded by Queen Charlotte as a recognition of the king's recovery (see Annex, entry for 15 April 1789). The king's brothers, William Henry, Duke of Gloucester, and Henry Frederick, Duke of Cumberland, attended this night, as did the king's eldest sons the Prince of Wales and Frederick Duke of York (in an uneasy display of loyalty), together with the bevy of young princesses who completed the queen's party.

THE ROYAL FAMILY AT THE THEATRES AND OPERA, 1760-1800

	DL	CG	K'S	HAY	PAN
George III and Queen Charlotte	262	299	98	28	3
Edward Augustus, Duke of York	0	1	0	0	0
William Henry, Duke of Gloucester	2	9	0	0	0
Henry Frederick, Duke of Cumberland	0	10	0	0	0
Prince Frederick William	0	1	0	0	0
Princess Augusta	1	7	0	0	0
Princess Louisa Ann	1	8	0	0	0
Princess Caroline Matilda	4	0	0	0	0
George Augustus Frederick, Prince of Wales	1	7	1	0	0
Frederick, Duke of York	1	6	0	0	0
William Henry, Duke of Clarence	1	2	0	0	0
Ernest Augustus, Duke of Cumberland	0	2	0	0	0
Total	273	352	99	28	3

Despite some interest in the plays of Elizabethan and Restoration writers, especially Shakespeare at the outset of the reign, we observe that George III and the members of his family continued the broad trend of the previous reign with a preference for contemporary plays, opera, and entertainments. The king himself took an especial delight in the works of Garrick, Colman, Murphy, Cumberland, Reynolds, Sheridan, and O'Keeffe, and the adaptations of the seventeenth century playwrights by Garrick and Colman. As so far recorded, in his reign the royal family witnessed thirty-seven performances from the sixteenth century and a mere twenty-seven from the seventeenth century, while one thousand and seventy-four were either contemporary compositions or adaptations.

TYPES OF ENTERTAINMENT ON ROYAL ATTENDANCE NIGHTS, 1760-1800

	C	T	F	HP	OP	BO	OR	PA/ENT
George III and Queen Charlotte	297	32	210	9	206	15	130	157
George Augustus, Duke of York	0	0	0	0	0	1	0	1
William Henry, Duke of Gloucester	5	2	3	2	4	0	0	7
Henry Frederick, Duke of Cumberland	2	3	2	1	1	2	0	6
Prince Frederick William	0	0	1	1	0	0	0	0
Princess Augusta	1	0	2	1	2	2	0	2
Princess Louisa Ann	3	1	3	2	2	1	0	5
Princess Caroline Matilda	1	2	0	1	0	0	0	2
George Augustus Frederick, Prince of Wales	5	0	3	0	3	0	0	5
Frederick, Duke of York	5	0	3	0	3	0	0	4
William Henry, Duke of Clarence	2	1	1	0	0	0	0	2
Ernest Augustus, Duke of Cumberland	0	2	1	0	0	0	0	1
Total	321	43	229	17	221	21	130	192

CHAPTER IV

VALUE OF ROYAL PATRONAGE
TO LONDON THEATRES, 1714-1800

The eighty-six years spanning the reigns of George I, George II, and the first two-thirds of George III's included more than three thousand, three hundred and twenty-five appearances at London playhouses, according to the record in *The London Stage*. Of this total the three kings attended on one thousand and eighty-one nights, the Princes of Wales eight hundred and sixty-two, and the remainder of the Royals one thousand two hundred and ninety-two. Unrecorded attendance should suggest a much larger number of nights, especially when, beginning with the accession of George III in 1760 (with the exception of twelve nights[1]), managements recorded only the 'Command' or presence of their Majesties. Others in his large family must have attended many times, since theatre-going was one of the chief entertainments of the time.[2] Nevertheless, this total attendance record should be sufficient to measure the support the Royals gave to the public theatres.

George I attended five entertainments (nine nights) written or composed in the sixteenth or early seventeenth century, but preferred fourteen (nineteen nights) from the Restoration period and seventy (ninety-seven nights) of contemporary productions. George II enjoyed eighteen plays (forty-two nights) from the early seventeenth century and forty-eight Restoration plays (seventy-nine nights), but attended seventy-nine contemporary productions (one hundred and eight nights). 'Poor Fred', Prince of Wales 1727-51, chose nineteen pre-Restoration entertainments (sixty-five nights), forty-six Restoration plays (one hundred and thirteen nights) and one hundred and ninety-eight contemporary entertainments (two hundred and forty-eight nights). His son, George III, preferred fifteen of the early plays (thirty-seven nights) to only seven from the Restoration (seventeen nights), while enjoying two hundred and forty-four contemporary productions (seven hundred and six nights) in the forty-year period under investigation, thus participating in the decline of the older pieces in favour of modern playwrights.

We have noted the taste of this influential group in each reign, but the grand totals included one thousand two hundred and five nights of comedy, nine hundred and sixty-eight of operas, four hundred and fifty-eight pantomime entertainments, four hundred and thirty-four farces, four hundred and twenty tragedies, two hundred and thirty-five ballad operas, one hundred and fifty-five oratorio nights, and one hundred and forty-seven evenings devoted to the plays of Shakespeare. Again their preferences were for comedy, music and light entertainment, rather than the serious forms of drama. Drury Lane Theatre was the most favoured house, having supported the Hanoverians consistently and entertained royalty on one thousand one hundred and eighty-four nights compared to eight hundred and fifty-four at the rival Covent Garden. The King's Theatre entertained them on eight hundred and thirty-six nights of opera, Lincoln's Inn Fields on one hundred and thirty-eight nights, and the Haymarket on one hundred and sixteen.

It is now possible to consider what such attendance contributed to the managements of these playhouses by way of the box-office, since much has been made of this influence by the critics. A. H. Scouten quotes an unknown writer in the *Grub Street Journal* for 8 April 1736 who stated that receipts on an ordinary night at Drury Lane, Covent Garden, and the Haymarket were £80, at Goodman's Fields £30 (which Scouten thinks is too low) - a total of £270 nightly.[3] G. W. Stone, Jr., quotes Garrick's own statement that a normally good Drury Lane house in the 1760's would bring in £120, but is content with a passing comment on the period 1747-1776: '...I have found but a single record during the period of nightly receipts dropping below £200 when Royalty was present.'[4] There follows my summary of receipts with approximate grosses (allowing for various alterations in the playhouses) at Lincoln's Inn Fields, Drury Lane, and Covent Garden over the eighty-six years (1714-1800) of the three reigns[5] - the largest and the smallest receipts on evenings 'By Command' or when other royalty was present.

ROYALTY AND THE BOX-OFFICE[6]

LIF (1714-1732)
£150 gross (4s/ 2s 6d/ 1s 6d/ 1s)
  Largest: £182   (2 December 1731)
  Smallest: £ 63 4s (11 November 1730)

DL (1714-1747)
£160 gross (4s/ 2s 6d/ 1s 6d/ 1s)
  Largest: £171   (31 May 1742)
  Smallest: £ 70   (11 March 1742)

(1747-62)
£231 gross (5s/ 3s/ 2s/ 1s)
  Largest: £220   (25 February 1758)
  Smallest: £150   (18 May 1759)

(1762-1775)
£354 gross (5s/ 3s/ 2s/ 1s)
  Largest: £270 4s (7 December 1774)
  Smallest: £175 7s (25 February 1773)

(1775-1780)
£354 gross (5s/ 3s/ 2s/ 1s)
  Largest: £335 3s 6d (21 March 1777)
  Smallest: £211 9s 6d (5 May 1775)

(1780-1794)
£600 gross (DL at K'S) (6s/ 3s 6d/ 2s)
  Largest: £319   0s 6d (5 October 1786)
  Smallest: £237 15s 6d (20 November 1782)

(1794-1800)
£770 gross (6s/ 3s 6d/ 2s/ 1s)
  Largest: £692 1s (1 February 1796)
  Smallest: £424   (20 February 1800)

CG (1732-1782)
   £200 gross (5s/ 3s 6d/ 2s/ 1s)
      Largest: £292 13s   (14 January 1780)
      Smallest: £ 35   7s 6d (16 April 1743)

(1782-1792)
   £325 gross (5s/ 3s 6d/ 2s/ 1s)
      Largest: £452 14s 6d (18 November 1789)
      Smallest: £264   1s   (27 February 1786)

(1792-1800)
   £481 gross (6s/ 3s 6d/ 2s/1s)
      Largest: £639 17s   (5 June 1799)
      Smallest: £261 18s 6d (18 December 1799)

It will be immediately apparent that on only five nights did the presence of royalty cause the admission receipts to exceed the house's gross. Was this because of the presence of the Royal Family or of the entertainment billed for those nights? At Lincoln's Inn Fields on 2 December 1713 the night's bill included Ravenscroft's *The Anatomist* with Theobald's *Apollo and Daphne,* an old play and a pantomime opera some five years old, 'For the Entertainment of Several Foreign Persons of Distinction' with the Duke of Lorraine present. At Drury Lane on 31 May 1742 Garrick played his famous *Richard III* before 'the Duke and Princesses Amelia, Caroline, and Louisa'. It was not until Covent Garden Theatre had undergone extensive alteration late in the century that its current gross was exceeded on 14 January 1780 with Goldsmith's *She Stoops to Conquer* and Bate's comic opera *The Flitch of Bacon;* on 18 November 1789 with Reynolds' new comedy *The Dramatist* and O'Keeffe's recent comic opera *The Highland Reel;* and on 5 June 1799 with Sheridan's *Pizzaro* (recently opened on 24 May) and Mrs. Inchbald's farce *The Wedding Day,* all By Command of their Majesties.

The other five nights failed to equal or exceed the gross of the house, but represent the largest receipts for their periods at Drury Lane Theatre. On 25 February 1758 the play was John

Home's *Agis* (opened on 21 February), a new tragedy with Garrick playing Lysander, attended by George William Frederick, the then Prince of Wales, and five of the Royal Family; on 7 December 1774 the play was the Fletcher-Buckingham-Garrick comedy *The Chances* 'for the 3rd time,' with Garrick as Don John, followed by Dibdin's *The Deserter;* on 21 March 1777 the oratorio *Messiah;* on 5 October 1786 a revival of Thomson's *Tancred and Sigismunda* with Sheridan's *The Critic;* and on 1 February 1796 O'Keeffe's *The Fugitive* with W. Linley's *Harlequin Captive* - all By Command of their Majesties.

Despite the largest receipts for the theatres on Command nights at each of these periods, even Royalty failed to muster an amount exceeding the gross for most of these nights. Perhaps this testimony will temper somewhat the excessive enthusiasm of those who like to think of the public's flocking to the playhouses to catch a glimpse of their King and/or other Royals or to be seen by other playgoers on Command nights. This may be at the root of Professor G.W. Stone's wry suggestion: '...the House of Hanover was prolific in births, and consequently subject to frequent demise. It is a pretty question whether losses from closed theatres during periods of official mourning were equalled by the extra take on nights of command performances, and by post-season bounties donated to the theatrical cause.'[7] Whatever the true situation, the record shows all three of the Royal Families loyally supporting the public playhouses diligently, and agreeing with the taste of their times by way of the Lord Chamberlain's suggestions or through their own devices.

NOTES
NOTES TO CHAPTER I

1   7 February 1704, *All for Love* (Dryden), for the Queen's birthday;
28 February 1704, *Sir Solomon Single* (Caryll);
24 April 1704, *The Merry Wives of Windsor* (Shakespeare);
5 February 1706, *The Anatomist* (Ravenscroft), for the Queen's birthday;
6 February 1707, *Camilla* (Buononcini-Haym), for the Queen's birthday.
After George of Denmark's death in 1708 the Queen ceased these celebrations. (Unless otherwise noted, all play titles and dates are taken from *The London Stage Part 2,* ed. Emmett L. Avery, 2 vols [Carbondale, Ill., 1960] - henceforward *L.S.2.* Play titles appear in various forms throughout the calendar, spelt in each case as on the daily playbills or newspaper advertisements.)

2   19 November 1703, Drury Lane, *The Constant Couple* (Farquhar), 'For the Entertainment of their Highnesses the Prince and Princess Landgrave of Hesse';
3 May 1706, Queen's Theatre, *The British Enchanters* (Grenville-Corbett), 'For the Entertainment of His Excellency Hamet Ben Hamet Cardenas, Ambassador from the Emperor of Fez and Morocco';
21 May 1706, Drury Lane, *Oroonoko* (Southerne), 'For the Entertainment of His Excellency Hamet Ben Hamet Cardenas';
25 April 1710, Drury Lane, *Aurengzebe* (Dryden), 'For the Entertainment of the Four Indian Kings';
27 April 1710, Queen's Theatre, *Hamlet* (Shakespeare-Davenant), 'For the Entertainment of the Four Kings lately arriv'd from America';
28 April 1710, Drury Lane, *Hydaspes* (Cicognini-Mancini), 'For the Entertainment of Four Indian Kings....' [Their names and nations, many syllables long, are then quoted in *L.S.2.* from the *Daily Courant* of 26 April.]

3   While few box-office receipts are available for the reign of George I, the following comment in *Colman's Opera Register* for the opera *Ernelinda* on 18 December 1714 is appropriate: 'Y^e Prince & Princess went to ye Play this night - ye Opera had but a thin House with Dancing.' The occasion was the opening of the new theatre in Lincoln's Inn Fields with *The Recruiting Officer* (Farquhar). Avery quotes receipts at Lincoln's Inn Fields that night of £143, and £82 for the same play on 20 December. *The Island Princess* (Motteux-Purcell-Clarke-Leveridge) on 10 March

1715 brought receipts of £154 18s. 6d. The average box-office receipt for 1714-15 was £69, and for 1715-16 only £33.

4   Thus 9 February 1750, Drury Lane, *Merope* (Hill), in *The London Stage Part 4,* ed. George Winchester Stone, Jr., 3 vols (Carbondale, Ill., 1961) [henceforward *L.S.4*], I, 173.

5   Thus 20 November 1793, Covent Garden, *The School for Arrogance* (Holcroft) *...Mother Shipton Triumphant* (Unknown), in *The London Stage Part 5,* ed. Charles Beecher Hogan, 3 vols (Carbondale, Ill., 1968) [henceforward *L.S.5*.], III, 1599.

6   **Princesses Anne and Amelia:**
     King's Theatre: *Rinaldo,* 27 January 1715 and 19 February 1715 (the latter, though, commanded for them by their father, the Prince of Wales);
     Drury Lane: *Love's Last Shift,* 19 March 1717 ('By Command', though whose is not stated - most likely the king's, as in all but one of these cases);
     Hampton Court: *The Stratagem,* 23 September 1718; *Henry VIII,* 1 October 1718.
     Princesses Anne, Amelia and Caroline:
     King's Theatre: *Arlequin Esprit Follet* and *Le Divorce*, 12 February 1719; *Arlequin Laron,* 5 March 1719; *Harlequin a Sham Astrologer,* 24 March 1720;
     Lincoln's Inn Fields: *The Merry Wives of Windsor,* 10 February 1724;
     King's Theatre: *Rodelinda,* 28 December 1725; *Elisa,* 15 January 1726; *Otho,* 8 March 1726; *Scipio,* 15 March 1726; *Alexander,* 31 May 1726.

7   So Baroness Ehrengard Melusia von Schulenberg.

8   Lady Louisa Stewart's *Anecdotes,* in Lady Mary Wortley Montague, *Letters,* ed. W.M. Thomas, 2 vols (London, 1861), I, xcv.

9   For the convention of actors' benefit nights see St Vincent Troubridge, *The Benefit System in the British Theatre* (The Society for Theatre Research, London, 1967); Allardyce Nicoll, *Early Eighteenth-Century Drama* (C.U.P., 1929), 286-7; *L.S.2,* I, xcviii.

10   *L.S.2,* II, 516 (entry for 26 Nov. 1718).

11   *Daily Post,* 18 March 1726 (*L.S.2,* II, 859).

12   See J.M. Beattie, 'The Court of George I and English Politics', *English Historical Review,* LXXXI, No.318 (January, 1966), 26-37.

13   See Graham Barlow, 'Hampton Court Theatre, 1718', *Theatre Notebook* xxxvii, No.2 (1983), 54-63.

14   *Apology* (London, 1889), II, 218.

NOTES TO CHAPTER II

1 *The London Stage Part 3,* ed. Arthur H. Scouten, 2 vols [henceforward *L.S.3*], I, 162.
2 *L.S.3,* I, 350.
3 *L.S.3,* I, 436.
4 *L.S.3,* II, 649.
5 *L.S.3,* I, 566. Fielding's political attacks in *Pasquin* and *The Historical Register for 1736* largely brought about Walpole's retaliation with the Licensing Act of 1737, which introduced repressive dramatic censorship (abandoned only in 1968). See Vincent J. Liesenfeld, *The Licensing Act of 1737* (Madison, Wis., 1984).
6 *L.S.3,* II, 660.
7 *L.S.3,* II, 1095.
8 *L.S.3,* I, 580.
9 *L.S.3,* I, 583.
10 *L.S.3,* II, 613.

NOTES TO CHAPTER III

1 *George III, His Court and Family,* 2 vols (London, 1820), I, 109-10.
2 J. Heneage Jesse, *Memoirs of the Life and Reign of George III,* 3 vols (London, 1867), II, 60.
3 Beckles Willson, *George III as Man, Monarch and Statesman* (London, 1907), 195-96.
4 John Clarke, 'The House of Hanover', *The Lives of the Kings and Queens of England,* ed. Antonia Fraser (London, 1977), ch. 8, p. 241.

NOTES TO CHAPTER IV

1 Twelve nights 'By Particular Desire':
Covent Garden: 2 January 1768, Dowager Princess of Wales and Duke of Cumberland; 4 January 1768, Duke of Gloucester; 7 January 1772, Dowager Princess of Wales and Duke of Gloucester; 8 January 1773, Duke of Cumberland; 12 June 1800, Prince of Wales, Duke of York, Duke of Clarence, Duke of Cumberland.
Drury Lane: 22 and 29 September and 1 and 11 October 1768, King of Denmark; 7 January 1772, Dowager Princess of Wales and Duke of Gloucester; 8 January 1773, Duke of Cumberland; 18 February 1773, Duke of Cumberland and Duke of Gloucester; 25 February 1773, Duke of Gloucester.
King's Theatre: 13 April 1782, Prince of Wales.

2   This is especially true in the case of George Augustus Frederick, Prince of Wales (the future George IV), whose famous affair with Mrs 'Perdita' Robinson began, according to popular report, with the performance of *The Winter's Tale* and *The Critic* at Drury Lane on 3 December 1779. The Prince was reported as immediately smitten by the lady's charms, and he began a back-stage pursuit of her. But the records do not show him in attendance on the following nights.

3   *L.S.3,* I, lxxiv.

4   *L.S.4,* I, liii.

5   The records for the Haymarket Theatre are missing.

6   The gross amount for the theatre in Lincoln's Inn Fields is approximated on the basis of Paul Sawyer's account of that playhouse: '...When John Rich left LIF... for Covent Garden he does not seem to have gained any seating capacity.... The pit certainly held more at Covent Garden than at LIF..., and probably both galleries held slightly more, but there was a considerable decrease in the seating capacity of the boxes' *(The New Theatre in Lincoln's Inn Fields* [The Society for Theatre Research, London, 1979], p. 16). The gross for Sheridan's first alteration at Drury Lane in 1780 is also estimated, while the grosses for both Drury Lane (1794-1800) and Covent Garden (1782-92, 1792-1800) are calculated from the figures derived from George Saunders and the latest prices of the box-office at both theatres: see Harry William Pedicord, *The Theatrical Public in the Time of Garrick* (New York, 1954), pp. 4-5.

7   *L.S.4.,* I, liii.

ANNEX

Royalty at the Play:
Comment and Contemporary Reports

This selection contains eye-witness reports and other comments made in connection with Hanoverian patronage of the theatre. The following conventions are used. In the cases of attendance, in the first entry the first item is the date of attendance, preceded by an asterisk if the performance is by royal command; then the theatre (see abbreviations below); the title of the main-piece in capitals, spelt as advertised for the night; in round brackets the author or librettist, and the composer if applicable, with the year of origin of the piece (except for the plays of Shakespeare); and lastly the type of production (see abbreviations below). The title, author etc., and type of the afterpiece, if any, constitute the entry immediately following. On a new line the name of the chief member of the royal party attending is next given; usually, further members of the royal family were also present, with ladies-in-waiting and equerries. Then follows the comment, and/or any contemporary report the source of which is normally the various volumes of *The London Stage 1660-1800* (see abbreviations below). Certain records do not relate to attendance but to other business associated with members of the royal family, of concern to the theatres: the dates of such records are enclosed in square brackets. Where appropriate, spelling and punctuation in the reports have been modernised.

Abbreviations used in Annex, Summary Tables, &c.

* : Command Performance.

Theatres:

CG : Covent Garden

DL : Drury Lane

HC : Hampton Court

K'S : King's Theatre

LIF : Lincoln's Inn Fields

PAN : Pantheon Theatre

RI : Richmond Theatre

SF : Southward Fair Booth

Type of Production:

BO or B/OP : ballad opera

BURL : burlesque

C : comedy

C/OP : comic opera

D/OP : dramatic opera

ENT : entertainment

F : farce

HP : history play

OP : opera

OR : oratorio

PA : pantomime

T : tragedy

The London Stage 1660-1800 (Carbondale, Ill., 1960-68):

L.S.2 : Part 2, 1700-1729, ed. Emmett L. Avery (2 vols)

L.S.3 : Part 3, 1729-1747, ed. Arthur H. Scouten (2 vols)

L.S.4 : Part 4, 1747-1776, ed. George Winchester Stone (3 vols)

L.S.5 : Part 5, 1776-1800, ed. Charles Beecher Hogan (3 vols)

ROYALTY AT THE PLAY:
Comment and Contemporary Reports

[1 Aug. 1714] Accession of George I to the throne of Great Britain and Ireland, the kingdom's first monarch of the House of Hanover, following the death of Queen Anne. King George I was crowned on 20 October 1714.

26 Oct. 1714 K'S   ARMINIUS (Unknown, 1714). OP.
King George I. First recorded attendance at King's Theatre by the new king.

*13 Dec. 1714 DL   THE TEMPEST (Shakespeare-Davenant-Dryden, 1667). C.
King George I. First recorded attendance at Drury Lane Theatre by the king.

*8 Jan. 1715 DL   THE OLD BATCHELOR (Congreve, 1693). C.
George Augustus, Prince of Wales, and Princess Caroline. The prince had notified the King's Theatre that he expected to be present at *Rinaldo,* but went to Drury Lane that night.

[19 Jan. 1715] King George I gave a Royal Patent to Sir Richard Steele for the Drury Lane company (PRO LC5/202-ff.280-85).

*10 Mar. 1715 LIF   THE ISLAND PRINCESS (Motteux-Purcell-Clarke-Leveridge, 1699). D/OP.
King George I. This night marked the first attendance of King George I at Lincoln's Inn Fields Theatre. The company was reputedly "Jacobite" in its political leanings, while Drury Lane advertised its loyalty to the new House of Hanover. *Weekly Packet,* 12 March: "His Majesty honoured that house [Lincoln's Inn Fields] with his presence the first time since they opened" [*L.S.2,* I, 346]. George I attended this playhouse only six times during his reign, all Command Performances.

6 Dec. 1716 DL   TAMERLANE (Rowe, 1701). T.
George Augustus, Prince of Wales. Assassination attempt. *Weekly Journal or British Gazetteer,* 8 December: "Last Thursday night his Royal Highness the Prince of Wales was at the theatre in Drury-Lane, when one Mr Freeman, a mad gentleman of £2000 per ann. offering to go into the boxes, and being stopped by one of the sentries in the passage, he shot him above the shoulder; however the sentry knocked him down, and securing him, 2 or 3 more loaded pistols were found in his pockets . . . . The sudden discharge of Mr Freeman's pistol put the ladies and others withinside the playhouse into some consternation at first . . . . The gentlemen about the prince, and almost throughout the

house, drew their swords upon the occasion of this disorder, which was soon over" [*L.S.2*, I, 425].

20 Sep. 1717 SF (ENTERTAINMENTS UNKNOWN) ENT.
George Augustus, Prince of Wales. The prince went to Penkethman's Booth at Southwark Fair, incognito. *Post Boy*, 26 September: ". . . [His Royal Highness] saw the droll at Penkethman's, and after at Bullock and Leigh's Booth" [*L.S.2*, I, 459].

[22 Apr. 1718] DL THE INDIAN EMPEROR (Dryden, 1665). T.
"By His Royal Highness's Command". *Original Weekly Journal*, 26 April, records the Prince of Wales as present this night, but Edward Harley, Jr., writing to Abigail Harley on 6 May stated:

> The P..., not long ago, bespoke at the old playhouse a play called *The Indian Emperor*. The K... hearing of it, sent to the players to tell them that if the P... came, and they acted that play, he would turn them out of his service, which message they sent to the P..., who had the good sense not to come, so *The Indian Emperor* was acted.
>
> --Portland MS, V, 560 [*L.S.2*, II, 491-2]

This must be an instance of the advice of the Lord Chamberlain, since King George could hardly have been so well read as to be able to recall the purport of Dryden's tragedy.

[29 Aug. 1718] Performances commanded at Hampton Court.
King George I. *Evening Post*, 30 August: "Yesterday Mr Bullock, master of the play-house in Lincoln's Inn Fields, was commanded to attend his Majesty at Hampton-Court, where he received orders for his company to perform several plays for the entertainment of his Majesty during his stay there, in the winter season, and there is a magnificent theatre erecting for that purpose." *Original Weekly Journal*, 30 August: "The king hath ordered the Comedians of the Theatre Royal in Drury-Lane to perform at Hampton-Court, during his Majesty's stay there, for which service they are to be allowed £100 extraordinary each night they act." [*L.S.2*, II, 502-3.]

*26 Nov. 1718 LIF LE MAITRE ETOURDI (from Molière, 1718). C.
LE TOMBEAU DE MAITRE ANDRE (Molière-de Barnete, 1718). PA.
King George I. William Byrd of Virginia attended this performance and noted ". . . where the French acted before the king and tumbled very well" [*The London Diary, 1717-21* (New York, 1958), p. 200]. *Original Weekly Journal*, 29 November: ". . . And we hear, his Majesty gave 100 guineas" [*L.S.2*, II, 516].

*6 Apr. 1719 DL   KING HENRY VIII (Shakespeare). HP.
King George I. Mrs Bicknell had announced previously *The Man of Mode* as the play for her benefit, but George I commanded *Henry VIII* instead.

[*20 Apr. 1719] DL   ALL FOR LOVE (Dryden, 1677). T.
[King George I.] The play scheduled for this night (Bickerstaff's benefit) had been *Henry VIII,* but the king commanded Dryden's tragedy. In the event George I was unable to attend. *Original Weekly Journal,* 25 April: "His Majesty was to have come to Drury Lane . . . but was prevented by the arrival of some important dispatches from abroad" [*L.S.2,* II, 536].

*22 Apr. 1719 LIF   SIR COURTLY NICE (Crowne, 1695). C.
King George I. Johnson's benefit had been advertised as *The Scornful Lady,* but the king's command replaced it with the Crowne comedy.

*25 Apr. 1719 LIF   JULIUS CAESAR (Shakespeare). HP.
King George I. Since *Julius Caesar* was never revised or adapted, and since both Drury Lane and Lincoln's Inn Fields included it in current repertoires, one may speculate as to why the latter theatre's production was favoured by George I on two occasions, instead of viewing the play at Drury Lane. The king seems to have preferred Quin (Brutus) and Ryan (Cassius) to Booth (Brutus) and Wilks (Antony). The repeat performance of *Julius Caesar* at Lincoln's Inn Fields attended by the king was on 9 April 1720.

*27 Apr. 1720 K'S   RADAMISTUS (Haym-Handel, 1720). OP.
King George I. *The Diary of Mary, Countess Cowper,* p. 154: "At night, *Radamistus,* a fine opera of Handel's making. The king was there with his ladies. The prince in the stage-box. Great crowd" [*L.S.2,* II, 578]. Mainwaring, *Handel,* pp. 98-99:

> If the persons who are now living, and who were present at the performance may be credited, the applause it received was almost as extravagant as his *Agrippina* had excited; the crowds and tumults of the house at Venice were hardly equal to those at London. In so splendid and fashionable an assembly of ladies (to the excellence of their taste we must impute it) there was no shadow of form, or ceremony, scarce indeed any appearance of order or regularity, politeness, or decency. Many, who had forced their way into the house with an impetuosity but ill-suited to their rank and sex, actually fainted through the heat and closeness of it. Several gentlemen were turned back, who had offered forty shillings for a seat in the gallery, after having despaired of getting any in the pit or boxes.   [*L.S.2,* II, 578]

*15 Apr. 1721 K'S   MUTIUS SCAEVOLA (Mattei-Buonocini-Handel, 1721). OP
King George I. De Fabrice to Flemming, 21 April (in Deutsch, *Handel,* p. 126): "The Princess of Wales was safely delivered of a son last Saturday. The news was taken to the king by Lord Herbert during . . . *Mutius Scaevola,* where there was a particularly large audience on account of its being the first performance. The audience celebrated the event with loud applause and huzzas . . ." [*L.S.2,* II, 624].

*17 Mar. 1726 LIF   THE COUNTRY WIFE (Wycherley, 1675). C.
APOLLO AND DAPHNE (Theobald-Galliard, 1726). PA.
King George I. *Daily Post,* 18 March: "His Majesty went . . . to see . . . *The Country Wife* and the entertainment of *Apollo and Daphne,* in which was performed a particular flying on that occasion, of a Cupid descending, and presenting his Majesty with a book of the entertainment, and then ascended: at which new piece of machinery the audience seemed much pleased" [*L.S.2,* II, 859].

   This was the last time recorded when George I attended a regular play put on by one of the patent companies, though he continued for more than a year to attend opera, and performances by the French *commedia dell' arte* troupe and the Italian Comedians, at the King's Theatre.

21 Apr. 1727 DL   THE RELAPSE (Vanbrugh, 1697). C.
HARLEQUIN'S TRIUMPH (Unknown, 1727). PA.
George Augustus, Prince of Wales, and Princess Caroline. Last recorded attendance as Prince and Princess of Wales.

*25 Apr. 1727 K'S   LA PARODIA DEL PASTOR FIDO (Unknown, 1727). ENT.
King George I. Last recorded attendance by George I.

[14 Jun. 1727] Accession of George Augustus as King George II, following the death of King George I. George II was crowned on 11 October 1727.

*28 Sep. 1727 DL   THE STRATAGEM (Farquhar, 1707). C.
King George II. First recorded appearance at the playhouse of George Augustus and Caroline as king and queen. Daily Post, 27 September: "*Macbeth* had been advertised for this day" [*L.S.2,* II, 935].

*11 Dec. 1728 DL   KING HENRY THE VIIITH (Shakespeare). HP.
HARLEQUIN DOCTOR FAUSTUS (J. Rich-Galliard, 1723). PA.
King George II. Also the Queen, Prince, Princess Royal, Princesses Amelia and Carolina. *Universal Spectator,* 14 December: "On Wednesday in the afternoon there was a riot at Drury-Lane Playhouse. The mob

hearing that their Majesties and the rest of the royal family were to be at the play in the evening, several disorderly people forced into the house pretending to keep places, broke and did a good deal of damage before they could be dislodged" [L.S.2, II, 1002].

This evening, with that of 28 January 1729 (at Drury Lane to see Shakespeare's *King Henry IV, Part 1),* and that of 6 March below, mark three of the rare occasions when we find King George II and his son Frederick Lewis, the new Prince of Wales ("Poor Fred"), together at the same theatre.

8 Jan. 1729 DL   LOVE IN A RIDDLE (C. Cibber-Unknown, 1729). B/OP.

Frederick Lewis, Prince of Wales. *Universal Spectator,* 11 January:

> Last Wednesday his Royal Highness the Prince went to . . . Drury-Lane to see Mr. Cibber's new pastoral . . . . The actors were for a while prevented from performing, by the great disturbance some of the audience made. But on a speech from Mr. Cibber, with a promise it should not be acted again, the catcalls, &c., ceased, and they were suffered to go on and end the same.   [L.S.2, II, 1007]

Is it possible that the prince had selected the piece, contrary to the expectations of the public?

*6 Mar. 1729 DL   SIR COURTLY NICE (Crowne, 1685). C.

King George II. *Daily Journal,* 7 March: "Last night the King, Queen, Prince of Wales, and the Princesses were all at the theatre in Drury-Lane . . . . But before the play began, a gentlewoman presented a book, addressed to Princess Amelia, entitled 'The Ladies Preservative, in the Three Chief Characteristicks of Beauty: the Hair, Complexion, and Teeth', which was very graciously received" [L.S.2, II, 1019].

*12 Nov. 1729 DL   THE INDIAN EMPEROR (Dryden, 1665). T. PERSEUS AND ANDROMEDA (Weaver?-Unknown, 1716). PA.

King George II. Of the latter title, Allardyce Nicoll points out that:

> Besides Theobald's piece [2 January 1730 at Lincoln's Inn Fields], there seem to have been no less than four entertainments of this name, one given at Drury lane in 1716, another at Drury Lane on 15 November 1728, another at Lincoln's Inn Fields, 18 November 1731.
>
> *--History of Early 18th-Century Drama,* p. 381.

Could the production of 15 November 1728 have been a revival or adaptation of Weaver's pantomime of 1716? It continued to be played at Drury Lane even on 2 January 1730 when Theobald's production opened at the new theatre in Lincoln's Inn Fields. Theobald's production, however, appears to have been a revival of an old entertainment, according to its playbill advertisement: "All the Characters new Drest, Likewise New Scenes, Machines and other Decorations." The king saw *Perseus and Andromeda* at Drury Lane this night (12 November 1729), and Theobald's version at Lincoln's Inn Fields on 18 November 1731.

20 Dec. 1732 CG   THE BEGGAR'S OPERA (Gay-Pepusch, 1728). B/ OP.
Frederick Lewis, Prince of Wales. The prince's first recorded appearance at the new Covent Garden Theatre. This was the fourth performance of *The Beggar's Opera* in a 20-day run of the revival featuring Miss Norsa, and the prince was to attend four other performances -- the 5th, 8th, 12th and 14th nights.

[20 Jan. 1733] Frederick Lewis, Prince of Wales. Henry Giffard made a bid for the prince's presence at the new Goodman's Fields Theatre, where he was billing *Love for Love* with Chetwood's *The Lover's Opera* -- or so we may surmise from *The Daily Advertiser,* 22 January: "Mr Giffard . . . gave a handsome entertainment and a concert of music to the company of Comedians [at Goodman's Fields] on occasion of his Royal Highness's birthday; also a bonfire, and a large quantity of liquor to the populace" [*L.S.3,* I, 265].

*25 Jan. 1733 DL   THE UNHAPPY FAVOURITE (Banks, 1681). T.
King George II. Lord Hervey wrote from St James's, 25 January 1733:

> In the evening I attended his Majesty to the Theatre in Drury Lane, where Mrs Porter played Queen Elizabeth most excellently (with a cane) for her own benefit, and to the fullest audience that ever was seen. The Dowager Dss of Marlborough was there with the Dss of Bedford and the Dss of Manchester. The Alpha and Omega of these three wept at the moving scenes. Tender creatures! And in one part of the play where Essex says,
>
> > 'Abhor all Courts, if thou art brave and wise,
> > For there thou never shalt be sure to rise.
> > Think not by doing well, a fame to get,
> > But be a villain, and thou shalt be great,'
>
> her Grace of Malborough cried charmingly, and clapped her hands so loud that we heard her [a]cross the theatre into the king's box.
> -- *Lord Hervey and his Friends,* ed. the Earl of Ilchester (London, 1950), 156-57.

*5 Nov. 1735 DL   TAMERLANE (Rowe, 1701). T.
King George II. Traditional performances of Rowe's play on 4 and 5 November each year had been neglected by the royal family. This date marks the first time recorded when the king and the royal family recognised the custom. The tragedy was intended to honour King William III and, by extension, the current monarch.

12 May 1736 CG   ATALANTA (Unknown-Handel, 1736). OP.
King George II. *Atalanta* was a new Handel opera written and performed "In Honour of the Royal Nuptials of their Royal Highnesses the Prince and Princess of Wales." *London Daily Post and General Advertiser,* 13 May:

> Last night was performed ... *Atalanta.* . . in which was a new set of scenes painted in honour to this happy union, which took up the full length of the stage: the fore-part of the scene represented an avenue to the Temple of Hymen, adorned with figures of several heathen deities. Next was a Triumphal Arch on the top of which were the arms of their Royal Highnesses, over which was placed a princely coronet. Under the arch was the figure of Fame, on a cloud, sounding the praises of this happy pair. The names Fredericus and Augusta appeared above in transparent characters. Through the arch was seen a pediment supported by four columns, on which stood two Cupids embracing, and supporting the feathers in a princely coronet, the royal ensign of the Prince of Wales. At the farther end was a view of Hymen's Temple, and the wings were adorned with the Loves and Graces bearing hymeneal torches, and putting fire to incense in urns, to be offered up upon this joyful union. The opera concluded with a Grand chorus, during which several beautiful illuminations were displayed . . . . There were present their Majesties, the Duke, and the four Princesses.
>
> [*L.S.3,* I, 583]

*30 Dec. 1736 DL   KING HENRY THE EIGHTH (Shakespeare). HP.
THE BURGOMASTER TRICK'D (Theobald-Galliard, 1726). PA.
Frederick Lewis, Prince of Wales. Discontent at King George II's long absence on the continent increased the prince's popularity. This night there were shouts of "Crown him! Crown him!" On 15 January 1737 the king returned to London. [*See* Vincent J. Liesenfeld, *The Licensing Act of 1737,* p. 69.]

[1 Jun. 1737] The Theatrical Licensing Act, passed in the House of Commons on this day, imposed censorship upon the theatres via the Lord Chamberlain's office.

28 Mar. 1738 K'S   AN ORATORIO, WITH A CONCERT ON THE ORGAN. OR.
Frederick Lewis, Prince of Wales. Benefit Handel. *London Evening Post,* 30 March: "Their Royal Highnesses the Prince and Princess of Wales were present; there was the greatest and most polite audience ever seen there, and it's thought Mr Handel could not get less that night than £1500." *Egmont Diary* (II, 474): "In the evening I went to Handel's Oratorio, where I counted near 1,300 persons besides the gallery and upper gallery. I suppose he got this night near £1,000." [*L.S.3,* II, 710.] The difference between these two estimates, supposing them to be well-informed, could be due to over-charges for seating and/or gifts to Handel.

*20 Jan. 1739 CG   MACBETH (Shakespeare-Davenant-Leveridge, 1702). D/OP.
PERSEUS AND ANDROMEDA (Theobald-Galliard, 1730). PA.
King George II. *London Daily Post and General Advertiser,* 22 January:

> Last Saturday night his Majesty, his Royal Highness the Duke, the Princesses, with several foreign ministers and their ladies were at [Covent Garden Playhouse]: so great a concourse of people came to see his Majesty there, as has scarcely been seen; many persons who came to the playhouse at four o'clock, offering any price, if they could possibly be admitted. In the Fury Dance of *Macbeth,* Mr Haughton had the misfortune to dislocate his ankle-bone, and fell down upon the stage, and was obliged to be carried off; upon which his Majesty was graciously pleased to send him ten guineas instantly, and to order him to be taken care of.
>
> [*L.S.3,* II, 756]

*21 Apr. 1741 DL   KING HENRY THE EIGHTH (Shakespeare). HP.
Frederick Lewis, Prince of Wales. The prince and princess were accompanied this night, and on the nights of 24 April (Buckingham's *Rehearsal* and the pantomime *Perseus and Andromeda)* and 15 May (Theobald's *Double Falsehood),* both at Covent Garden Theatre, by four-year-old Lady Augusta and by Prince George William Frederick (three years old), the future King George III.

[20 Mar. 1751] Death of Frederick Lewis, Prince of Wales. Subsequently his son, George William Frederick, was proclaimed Prince of Wales.

*29 Nov. 1757 CG   SHE WOU'D AND SHE WOU'D NOT (C. Cibber, 1702). C.
A DUKE AND NO DUKE (Tate, 1684). F.
King George II. Last recorded theatrical attendance by George II.

[25 Oct. 1760] Death of King George II. The theatres were closed for a three-week period; previously the closure on the death of a monarch had been for six weeks [*L.S.4,* II, 824]. George William Frederick acceded as King George III on his grandfather's death, and was crowned on 22 September 1761.

*21 Nov. 1760 DL   KING RICHARD III (Shakespeare-C. Cibber, 1699). HP.
King George III. First recorded attendance of George William Frederick as George III. *Walpole* to Montague, 24 November:

> The first night the king went to the play, which was civilly on a Friday, not on the opera night, as he was used to do, the whole audience sang *God Save the King* in chorus. For the first act, the press was so great at the door that no ladies could go to the boxes, and only the servants appeared there, who kept places: at the end of the second act the whole mob broke in and seated themselves; yet all this zeal is not likely to last, though he well deserves it.
>
> [*L.S.4,* II, 825]

Garrick played Richard in his first Command Performance before George III as king. Garrick wrote to George Colman: "I received this at noon but pray let me see *you* after the play -- if the king comes to Richmond I shall go to bed, if not Hubert will call upon me with you at Southampton Street --" [*The Letters of David Garrick,* ed. Little and Kahrl, I, 331].

*12 Dec. 1760 DL   THE REHEARSAL (Buckingham-Garrick, 1742). BURL.
POLLY HONEYCOMBE (Colman, 1760). F.
King George III. *Gazetteer and London Daily Advertiser,* 13 December: "At fifteen minutes past six, his Majesty went to D--L-- House, attended by several great officers of state, to see *The Rehearsal* and *Polly Honeycombe* . . . . The bills were stuck up [in the] morning for only *The Rehearsal,* but about ten o'clock a message was sent, signifying his Majesty's pleasure to have the new dramatic novel of *Polly Honeycombe* added to it; upon which fresh bills were printed and pasted up . . ." [*L.S.4,* II, 830].

*23 Dec. 1760 DL   KING JOHN (Shakespeare-Garrick, 1745). HP.
King George III. *Charlotte Fermor* to Countess of Pomfret: "The king is gone to the play, which is *King John;* he has hardly ever bespoke any other than Shakespeare's historical plays, all of which they say he has ordered to be revived, and takes great pleasure in" [*L.S.4,* II, 833]. Later in his life, though, George III confided to Fanny Burney that he found much of Shakespeare "sad stuff -- only one must not say so!" -- a statement much quoted as evidence that the king either was, or was not, out of his mind.

*14 Sep. 1761 DL   THE REHEARSAL (Buckingham-Garrick, 1742).
BURL.
King George III. Garrick had officially acknowledged a royal command
for *The Rehearsal,* writing on 30 July 1761:

> His Grace the Duke of Devonshire has informed me of his
> Majesty's most gracious intention in favour of the managers of his
> theatre.
>
> I find myself unable to describe my feelings for the great honour
> that is done to us, or to express my acknowledgments for your
> Lordship's goodness and protection.
>
> All that I can do is to assure your Lordship that I will, as I have
> ever done, most zealously exert the little talents I have for his
> Majesty's entertainment. It is my chief ambition, as well as duty,
> to obey the commands I shall be honoured with, to the utmost of
> my ability.
>
> *[Letters of David Garrick,* I, 343-4]

[19 Nov. 1761] King George III. Garrick wrote this day to Sir Joshua
Reynolds to inform him that ". . . he is likewise obliged to disengage
himself every Thursday to wait the commands of the king, and Friday is
the day he has hitherto performed upon. . ." *[Letter of David Garrick,* I,
346]. Beginning with the season of 1761-62, all command performances
were scheduled for Thursdays.

[9 Nov. 1765] King George III. Garrick wrote to Richard Berenger before
this date as follows:

> . . . And therefore I had determined from necessity to give up
> acting. . . . This Sir was my resolution, which can only be broke
> through by a command; which my duty, my pride, my
> inclination, and my gratitude, will always make me obey. . . .

According to David M. Little and George M. Kahrl, the editors of
Garrick's letters, Garrick wrote to Berenger because he was a member
of the royal household. The letter was answered by Nicholas Ramus,
Senior Page of the Backstairs, who was in charge of the king's
entertainment selections. To his brother George, Garrick wrote:

> His Majesty has desired me to appear again to oblige him and the
> Queen. I shall obey their commands, but only for a few
> nights. . . .
>
> *[Letters of David Garrick,* II, 476-7]

*12 Jan. 1769 DL   KING RICHARD III (Shakespeare-C. Cibber, 1699). HP.
THE PADLOCK (Bickerstaffe-C. Dibdin, 1768). C/OP.
King George III. *Neville Diary:*

> Garrick played Richard III. In attempting to get into the pit was forced into the two-shilling gallery passage, and after being squeezed abominably for an hour got into the street. Should not have received much pleasure if I had got in, as that calf-headed son of a whore, George &c, was there.

> [*L.S.4,* III, 1379]

*10 Mar. 1775 DL   JUDAS MACCABAEUS (Morell-Handel, 1748). OR.
King George III. *Westminster Magazine,* March 1775:

> On Friday the third instant the entertainments peculiar to this season commenced. Messrs. Bach and Abel were first, and have been at each successive oratorio since (one night excepted when the king and queen favoured Mr Stanley, with bringing the only good house he has hitherto had), honoured with the presence of their Majesties, who have been accused, we think justly, of partiality to these foreigners, in overlooking Mr Stanley's past services and great personal merits. Justice, however, requires us to observe, that both in point of vocal and instrumental performers, the former have displayed a striking superiority over the latter.

> [*L.S.4,* III, 1875]

*6 Feb. 1786 DL   THE WAY TO KEEP HIM (Murphy, 1760). C.
THE VIRGIN UNMASK'D (Fielding-Unknown, 1735). B/OP.
King George III. ". . . As soon as Mrs Siddons had recovered from her lying-in, we find the king ordering Murphy's comedy, *The Way to Keep Him,* in which the great actress performed the part of Mrs. Lovemore. . ." [J.H. Jesse, *Memoirs of George Selwyn and his Contemporaries* (Boston, 1902), III, 2].

*15 Apr. 1789 CG   HE WOU'D BE A SOLDIER (Pilon, 1786). C.
ALADIN (Locke, 1789). PA.
Queen Charlotte. "By Command of Her Majesty." George III had been ill (with porphyria, as is now known) and suffering a mental breakdown since the previous November, but was now recovering rapidly. This was the first public appearance by members of the royal family since the onset of the king's illness. A report is given in *L.S.5,* II, 1146:

The drop curtain with the king's arms on it shown when the front curtain first rose was the "original curtain exhibited on the opening of Lincoln's Inn Fields theatre [in 1714]. . . . It has lain by in the scene-room of Covent-Garden theatre nearly seventy years, but was rescued from oblivion, retouched, and the appropriate ornaments added for the occasion" (*Public Advertiser,* 16 April).

On the queen's entrance "the house called for *God Save the King,* and the theatre being prepared, the song was immediately sung by Bannister, Johnstone, and Darley, the house joining in the chorus. It was encored. . . . At the end of the play [it] was again called for, and again sung twice. At the end of the pantomime it was again called for; and the theatre not sending forward the performers, the audience cheerfully sung it for themselves; and having sung, they encored themselves; so that altogether it was sung six times in the course of the evening. Her Majesty had a bandeau of black velvet, on which were set in diamonds the words 'Long live the king'. The princesses had bandeaus of white satin, and 'Long live the king' in gold" (*Universal Magazine,* April 1789, p. 218).

[21 Apr. 1789] K'S   A GALA (sponsored by Brooks's Club). ENT.
Held in celebration of the recovery of King George III. From *L.S.5,* II, 1148:

Shortly before midnight an overture was played, followed by a duet sung by Kelly and Sga Storace, assisted by a chorus, with music by Mazzinghi. An Ode, written by Robert Merry, was then recited by Mrs Siddons, dressed "à la Britannia, with a spear, standing on a raised stage. . . . This being finished a transparent painting dropped upon her, and she was no more seen." The Ode was concluded at 12.30, and *Rule Britannia* was sung. Supper was served at two o'clock, but no dancing was possible because of the large number of guests. "Many persons were not gone at six in the morning." The price of seven tickets was 25 guineas. (*World,* 22, 23 April.)

[24 Apr. 1789] (A GENERAL THANKSGIVING)
A public thanksgiving for the recovery of King George III closed the theatres. DL playbill of 23 April: "There will be no Performance Tomorrow Evening on Account of the Illuminations" [*L.S.5,* II, 1148].

*16 Dec. 1789 DL   THE HAUNTED TOWER (Cobb, 1789). C/OP.
WHO'S THE DUPE? (Mrs Cowley, 1779). F.
King George III. From *L.S.5,* II, 1214:

World, 19 December: *God Save the King* was sung "by the performers and by the audience five times: twice on the entrance of the king and queen, once after the play, twice after the farce".

Account-Book, Richard Peake, sub-treasurer: "In the pit of this night 525 persons; this is the greatest number ever remembered to be in at any one time".

[23 Apr. 1790] DL   LOVE FOR LOVE (Congreve, 1695). C.
THE PANNEL (Kemble, 1788). F.
Honouring the anniversary of King George III's recovery. (See 24 April 1789, above.) As quoted in *L.S.5,* II, 1247, the advertisement ran:

Previous to mainpiece, this being the anniversary of his Majesty's happy recovery, *British Loyalty; or, a Squeeze for St. Paul's* by Bannister Jun. After which, the stage being decorated and illuminated in the same superb style which it was for the reception of his Majesty on Dec. the 16 last, *God Save the King* by Dignum, Sedgwick, Alfred, Danby, Fawcett, Haymes, Hollingsworth, Lyons, Maddocks, Phillimore.

*22 Feb. 1791 PAN   ARMIDA (Gamerra-Sacchini-others, 1791). OP.
King George III. The Pantheon Theatre was in Oxford Street. When *Armida* had opened in the newly-converted Pantheon on 17 February, the acoustics and the conduct of the performance were severely criticised. Not only were the performers considered imperfect, but even the scene-shifters, despite the advertised fiat that "by command of his Majesty no person can be admitted behind the scenes during the performance" [*L.S.5,* II, 1323]. There was a poor house for the command performance on 22 February. *L.S.5,* II, 1325 quotes the *Morning Chronicle* of 23 February:

There were not an hundred persons in the pit when their Majesties entered, and there were not double the number at any part of the evening. The royal box being in the centre, fronting the stage, their Majesties were invisible to the gallery; and on their entrance solemn stillness prevailed, until the orchestra, for the first time in an opera-house, for the first time by the professional band, struck up *God Save the King.* Never, we will venture to say, in any theatre during the present reign, was there so thin an audience when their Majesties were present; and we pretend not to divine the cause. Whether it is the failure of the theatre as a musical room -- the general poverty of the performance -- the little notice that was given of their Majesties' intention to be present, we know not.

[*23 Jan. 1793] CG   NOTORIETY (Reynolds, 1791). C.
HARLEQUIN'S MUSEUM (Unknown, 1792). PA.
King George III. Morning Chronicle, 24 January: "*Notoriety* and *Tom Thumb* were to have been performed by command of their Majesties; but, in consequence of the news from France [execution of Louis XVI on 21 January], at five o'clock a letter was received from the vice-chamberlain, stating that their Majesties could not honour the theatre with their presence, and the farce was changed from *Tom Thumb* to the new pantomime" [*L.S.5*, III, 1515].

*1 Feb. 1796 DL   THE FUGITIVE (O'Keeffe, 1790). C.
HARLEQUIN CAPTIVE (W. Linley, 1796). PA.
King George III. On the royal party's return from Drury Lane Theatre this evening via Pall Mall to Buckingham House, a stone was thrown at the royal coach. King George and Queen Charlotte and a lady-in-waiting were unhurt.

*15 May 1800 DL   SHE WOU'D AND SHE WOU'D NOT (C. Cibber, 1702). C.
THE HUMOURIST (Cobb, 1784). F.
King George III. On this day three separate and uncoordinated incidents put the king's well-being in peril. The morning saw the accidental discharge of a musket when the king was conducting a military review. The king was shot at during an assassination attempt at the theatre in the evening. There was a molestation of the royal carriage on the way home at night. Attention is drawn in *L.S.5*, III, 2274, to the description of this trying day in the life of the king in *The Gentleman's Magazine* (vol. 70, pt. 1, May 1800, 478-480). That description is worth airing in full here, as a fitting if more than usually dramatic episode to round off this record of eighteenth-century royalty at the play:

> Domestic Occurrences, May 16.
>
> We have authority to state, that the misfortune which happened yesterday morning, at the field-day of the Grenadier battalion of Guards, in Hyde-park, arose entirely from accident. A due regard to the anxiety that every individual of the battalion feels that this matter should be properly understood is our inducement for giving this statement to the public.
>
> The coincidence of this event, with the atrocious attempt at night in the theatre, tended to strengthen an opinion, previously entertained by some, that it was not entirely the effect of accident, but arose from a design against his Majesty's sacred person. There is not the least reason, however, to suppose that this was the case. The king was within twenty yards of the battalion, and about

The HORRID ASSASSIN, I.^s HATFIELD, attempting to Shoot the KING in Drury Lane Theatre—on the 15 of May 1800.

Plate 2

Reproduced by courtesy of the Trustees of the British Museum.

(See note on this illustration, p. vii)

eight yards, upon a parallel line, from the gentleman who was wounded. His Majesty was on horseback; and the musket that fired the ball must not only have been pointed low, but could not have been directed against his person, otherwise it could not have missed him by so many yards, and hit a gentleman not standing behind, but in the same line with him.

Every loyal heart must be filled with grief and indignation on hearing of the danger to which his Majesty's sacred life was afterwards exposed, and from which he so providentially escaped.

The king and queen, and the Princesses Augusta, Elizabeth, Mary, and Amelia, with their usual attendants, honoured the theatre with their presence, to see the comedy of "She Wou'd and She Wou'd Not", and the farce of "The Humourist". Just as his Majesty entered his box, and while he was bowing to the audience with his usual condescension, a person who sat in the second row from the orchestra, but towards the middle of the pit, stood up, and levelling a horse-pistol towards the king's box, fired it.

It was so instantaneous as to prevent all the persons near him from seeing his design in time to defeat it, though we learn that, providentially, a gentleman who sat next to him, Mr Holroyd, of Scotland Yard, had the good fortune to raise the arm of the assassin, so as to direct the contents of the pistol towards the roof of the box.

The audience remained for a few seconds in a mute agony of suspense. The queen was about making her entry; and the curtain rising, as generally arranged on such occasions, his Majesty, with the greatest presence of mind and tenderness, waved his hand as a signal to dissuade his royal consort from her immediate appearance; and, instantly standing erect, raised his right hand to his breast, and continued for some time in a bowing attitude to the spectators, to remove their perturbation of mind for his safety. Her Majesty now entered, and appeared to be much agitated, clasping her hands with great emotion. On the entry of the princesses the confusion attendant upon the outrage had not subsided; and, on being informed of the cause, Augusta fainted away, but was soon recovered by the tender attentions of her sister Elizabeth, and the ladies in waiting. By this time, however, the Princess Mary became no less affected at the alarming communication, and the same means to effect her recovery were, with equal success, had recourse to.

After the first moment of stupor, the persons around him, and some musicians from the orchestra, seized the man, and hurried him over the pallisades into the music-room. Mr Wright, a solicitor in Wellclose Square, who sat immediately behind him, was the first to secure him. He dropped the pistol, but Mr Wright found it under the seat.

The affecting scene being at length terminated, by the entire composure of the royal females, "God Save the King" was twice sung, amidst the most enthusiastic shouts of true loyalty and affection.

The play then commenced. Mr Bannister first came on, and attempted to proceed; but was interrupted by the audience, who eagerly enquired whether the assassin was in safe custody; at the same time insisting that he should be brought upon the stage. Mr Bannister answered, that the villain certainly was in custody; Mrs Jordan soon after came forward also, and assured the house of the same fact. The audience now became perfectly satisfied, and the performances were suffered to go on without any further interruption.

At the end of the farce, "God Save the King" was again demanded; and the following stanza (originally composed *impromptu* at Quebec) was sung as the concluding verse: it is needless to observe, that it was received with enthusiastic applause, and encored:

> From every latent foe,
> From the assassin's blow,
>   God shield the king!
> O'er him Thine arm extend,
> For Britain's sake defend
> Our father, prince, and friend:
>   God save the King!

The royal party then left the theatre amidst the prayers and plaudits of the crowded circle, who, while they thus manifested their sincere regard for a most virtuous and gracious sovereign, sufficiently marked their indignation at the conduct of the treasonable assassin, who basely dared to aim a blow at the life of a prince so justly endeared to all his people.

When the king's carriage, on the way home, came to the corner of Southampton Street, a person, by trade a shoe-maker, who it seems had placed himself there for that purpose, hooted and hissed his Majesty in the most impudent and audacious manner, and continued following his carriage for some time, displaying every mark of contempt and disrespect, till at length he was taken into custody.

When the royal family reached the Queen's House, supper was immediately brought up, but none of the royal family sat down. Her Majesty drank a glass of wine and water, and then retired. The Princess Amelia, who has been ill near two years, fainted on entering her chamber; and the fits continued so long, that her restoration to life appeared doubtful. His Majesty, who was during the whole evening perfectly cool and collected, on hearing of the situation of Amelia, went to her Royal Highness's chamber, and attended her until recollection returned, when she threw herself into the king's arms, and said, "She would be comforted". His Majesty, on leaving the chamber of Amelia, went to Elizabeth, Mary, and Augusta, whose situation was nearly the same as the Princess Amelia's; but a great show of tears brought them relief, in which state they passed the night. During this scene of confusion, the Princess Sophia (who has been for some time indisposed) repeatedly called to her attendant to know the cause of it. She said that the Princess Amelia had returned from the theatre ill. His Majesty, on passing, said "Sophia, good night", and retired to rest: it was then one o'clock.

We now proceed to state, as accurately as possible, what followed the apprehending of the traitor. The Duke and Duchess of York were in their box at the time; and his Royal Highness, who was an eye-witness of the transaction, immediately left it, and attended the examination of the offender in the room into which he had been conducted, and where he had been searched to see if he had any other fire-arms, or papers. He had none. Mr Tamplin, a trumpeter in the band, who assisted in taking him over the orchestra [sc. orchestra-pit "pallisades"], recognised the man to be a soldier, and pulling open his coat, found that he had on a military waistcoat, with the button of the Fifteenth Light Dragoons. It was an old officer's waistcoat.

On being questioned by Mr Sheridan [viz. R.B. Sheridan, proprietor of the theatre], he said, "He had no objection to tell who he was -- it was not over yet -- there was a great deal more and worse to be done. His name was James Hadfield; he had served his time to a working silversmith, but had enlisted into the Fifteenth Light Dragoons, and had fought for his king and country." At this time the Prince of Wales and Duke of York entered the room. He immediately turned to the Duke, and said, "I knew your Royal Highness -- God bless you! I have served with Your Highness, and --" (pointing to a deep cut over his eye, and another long scar on his cheek, said) "-- I got these, and more than these, in fighting by your side. At Lincelles I was left three hours among the dead in a ditch, and was taken prisoner by the French. I had my arm broken by a shot, and eight sabre wounds in my head; but I recovered, and here I am."

He then gave the following account of himself and of his conduct, and he said that having been discharged from the army, on account of his wounds, he had returned to London, and now lived by working at his own trade. He made a good deal of money: he worked for Mr Hougham, of Aldersgate Street. Being weary of life, he last week bought a pair of pistols of one William Wakelin, a hairdresser and broker, in St John Street. (Mr Sheridan and Mr Wigstead immediately sent persons to bring Wakelin to the theatre.) He told him, they were for his young master, who would give him a blunderbuss in exchange. [Hadfield continued:] That he had borrowed a crown from his master that morning, with which he had bought some powder, and had gone to the house of Mrs Mason, in Red Lion Street, to have some beer; that he went backwards to the yard, and there he tried his pistols. He found one of them good for nothing, and left it behind him. In his own trade he used lead, and he cast himself two slugs, with which he loaded his pistol, and came to the theatre.

At this part of his narrative Sir William Addington arrived; and taking the chair, went over the examination of the persons who had secured him, and who had seen the pistol levelled at his Majesty. Sir William said it was most material to ascertain the fact whether the pistol was levelled at the sacred person of his Majesty, or fired at random; as the one case would be high treason, the other not. He asked Hadfield what had induced him to attempt the life of the best of sovereigns. He answered that he had not attempted to kill the king; he had fired his pistol over the royal box; he was as good a shot as any in England; but he was himself weary of life; he wished for death, but not to die by his own hands; he was desirous to raise an alarm; but wished that the spectators might fall upon him; -- he hoped that his own life was forfeited. He was asked if he belonged to the Corresponding Society [of radicals and republicans, a movement made illegal by the

Corresponding Societies Act of 1799]. He said no, he belonged to no political society; but that he belonged to a club called the *Odd Fellows,* and that he was a member of a benefit society. And being asked if he had any accomplices, he solemnly declared that he had none, and with great energy took God to witness, and laid his hand on his heart.

From this time he began to show manifest signs of mental derangement. When asked who his father was, he said he had been the postillion to some duke, but could not say what duke. He talked in a mysterious way of dreams, and of a great commission he had received in his sleep; that he knew he was to be a martyr, and was to be prosecuted [*sic*] like his great master, Jesus Christ. He had been persecuted in France; but he had not yet been sufficiently tried. He said many other incoherent things in the same style.

William Wakelin, the person of whom he had bought the pistols, being brought to the house was examined. He said it was true that he had bought a pair of pistols of him, and that he had said they were for his young master, who would give him a blunderbuss for them; but he had not yet got the blunderbuss. He knew very little of Hadfield, but knew where he worked, and had heard a good character of him, but that the least drink affected his head. Several persons from the house of Mrs Mason, his acquaintance, confirmed this fact; and they said they ascribed this to the very severe wounds he had received in the head. The least drink quite deranged him.

On this evidence he was committed to Cold Bath Fields, for re-examination; and the Dukes of Clarence and Cumberland, and Mr Sheridan, conducted him thither. His Majesty's Privy Council, however, offering to examine him forthwith to discover if he had any accomplices, he was taken to the Duke of Portland's office where he underwent another examination. Mr Wright, Mr Holroyd, Mr Tamplin, Mr Calkin, Mr Parkinson, Mr Francis Wood, Mr Lion, and Mr Dietz, the persons who were instrumental in securing him, and whose evidence is the most material as to his directing the pistol toward his Majesty's box, if not towards his sacred person, also attended.

After this the Duke of Clarence, Duke of Cumberland, Mr Sheridan, and a number of officers, went back to the theatre; and, after their Majesties had withdrawn, the most strict search was made for the slugs. A mark was discovered in the top of the canopy over the royal box, and, in the orchestra below, a flattened and irregular piece of lead was found, supposed to have recoiled from the place where it struck. It was providential that at this theatre the royal box is elevated more than fifteen feet above the pit; so that from the place where Hadfield levelled his pistol, he was between thirty and forty feet distant from his Majesty's person.

The Prince of Wales, who was at dinner at Lord Melbourne's, was almost immediately informed of the circumstances by Mr Jefferys, M.P. for Coventry; who, thinking a variety of erroneous reports might reach his Royal Highness, instantly left the theatre, where he had been an eye-witness of the circumstance, to inform the prince of it, and of the king's safety. His Royal Highness immediately went to the theatre to attend his Majesty.

A few further details can be added to this account from later sources.

Social historians of George III's reign suggest that the firing of the bullet at the Guards' review was not, perhaps, the accident for which it was dismissed. It may have been an actual attempt at assassination from some unknown source, because subsequent examination of the guardsmen's cartridge-boxes appeared to establish that they had been issued with nothing but blanks.

Henry Wigstead was one of the Middlesex magistrates; Sir William Addington was a Westminster magistrate, from the Bow Street office. They both had theatrical sympathies. Wigstead, an amateur limner and caricaturist, is on record as having "collected" views for the scenery prepared for William Pearce's *Hartford Bridge* (Covent Garden, 1792). William Addington was thought to be the author of a play, *The Prince of Agra* (Covent Garden, 1774), and was "fond of going behind the scenes". Richard Brinsley Sheridan, dramatist, parliamentarian, and proprietor of Drury Lane Theatre, was on duty that night to escort the royal party to their box. Biographers of Sheridan aver that upon the shooting, it was he who delayed the entrance of the queen and princesses until the disturbance was under control, improvising the excuse that a pickpocket was being apprehended in the pit; learning this, the grateful king invited Sheridan, Mrs Sheridan and eldest son Tom to court on the morrow. It is also claimed for Sheridan that it was he who immediately "dashed off" the additional stanza of the royal anthem.

Hadfield was tried at the Court of King's Bench on 26 June. The judge, Lord Justice Kenyon, stopped the case on the overwhelming evidence of Hadfield's derangement, and acquitted him as insane. Hadfield was committed first to Newgate and then to Bedlam, where, after a couple of short-lived escapes, he eventually died.

Sheridan ordered special silver medals to be struck to commemorate the king's escape. On one side the words *GOD SAVE THE KING* encircle a shield and shivered arrows, meant to represent providence protecting the king from the attempt on his life. On the other side the British crown is surrounded by a wreath of laurel, on the knot of which appears *Give God Praise;* the main motto is *Preserved from Assassination, May 15, 1800:* and, in the words of one enthusiast for the medal's ultimate sublimity, "radiant beams of glory spread their influence over all".

[Allardyce Nicoll, *Late Eighteenth-Century Drama* (1937), pp. 29, 232; Percy Fitzgerald, *Chronicles of Bow Street Police Office* (1888), I, 17 and II, 8; Lewis Gibbs, *Sheridan* (1947), pp. 202-3; Oscar Sherwin, *Uncorking Old Sherry* (1960), pp. 273-5; John Clarke, *The Life and Times of George III* (1972), pp. 168-9; John Ashton, *The Dawn of the Nineteenth Century in England* (1886), pp. 8-12.]

BIBLIOGRAPHY

Including sources drawn on for *The London Stage 1660-1800, Pts. 2, 3, 4 and 5.*

Anon. *George III, his Court and Family.* 2 vols. London, 1820.

Ashton, John. *The Dawn of the Nineteenth Century in England.* London, 1886.

Baldwin's London Journal; or, British Chronicle. London, 1762-92.

Barlow, Graham. "Hampton Court Theatre, 1718", in *Theatre Notebook* xxxvii, no. 2. London, 1983.

Beattie, J.M. "The Court of George I and English Politics", in *English Historical Review* lxxxi, no. 318. London, 1966.

Biographia Dramatica; or, A Companion to the Playhouse. By David Erskine Baker, Isaac Reed, and Stephen Jones. 2 vols in 4 pts. London, 1812.

Biographical Dictionary of Actors, Actresses, etc., A. By Philip H. Highfill, Jr., Kalman A. Burnim, and Edward A. Langhans. Carbondale, Ill., 1973 --.

Byrd, William. *The London Diary, 1717-1721.* New York, 1958.

Chetwood, William Rufus. *A General History of the Stage.* London, 1749.

Cibber, Colley. *An Apology for the Life of Mr Colley Cibber.* Ed. Robert W. Lowe. 2 vols. London, 1889.

Cibber, Theophilus. *Theophilus Cibber to David Garrick, Esq. With Dissertations on Theatrical Subjects.* London, 1759.

Clarke, John. *The Life and Times of George III.* London, 1972.

------. "The House of Hanover", in *The Lives of the Kings and Queens of England.* Ed. Antonia Fraser. London, 1977.

Critical Balance of Performers at Drury Lane Theatre, A. London, 1765.

Critical Review, The. Ed. Tobias Smollett. London, 1759.

Davies, Thomas. *Dramatic Miscellanies.* 3 vols. Dublin, 1784.

------. *Memoirs of the Life of David Garrick, Esq.* 2 vols. London, 1780.

------. ------. Rev. ed. Stephen Jones. London, 1808.

Derrick, Samuel. *The Dramatic Censor.* London, 1752.

Dircks, Richard J. "Garrick and Gentleman: Two Interpretations of Abel Drugger", in *RECTR.* November 1968.

Dramatic Censor, The: Being Remarks on the Conduct, Character, and Catastrophe of our Most Celebrated Plays. By several Hands. London, 1752.

Drury Lane Calendar 1747-1776. Ed. Dougald MacMillan. Oxford, 1938.

Fitzgerald, Percy. *The Life of David Garrick.* 2 vols. London, 1878. Rev. ed. 1899.

------. *Chronicles of Bow Street Police Office.* 2 vols. London, 1888.

Gazetteer and London Daily Advertiser, The. London, 1741-96.

Genest, John. *Some Account of the English Stage from the Restoration in 1660 to 1830.* 10 vols. Bath, 1832.

Gentleman, Francis. *The Dramatic Censor; or, Critical Companion.* 2 vols. London, 1770.

Gentleman's Magazine, The. Ed. E. Cave, &c. London, 1731--.

Gibbs, Lewis. *Sheridan.* London, 1947.

Gray, Charles H. *Theatrical Criticism in London to 1795.* New York, 1931.

Haig, R. L. *The Gazetteer, 1715-1797.* Carbondale, Ill., 1960.

Hawkins, William. *Miscellanies in Prose and Verse.* London, 1775.

Lord Hervey and His Friends. Ed. the Earl of Ilchester. London, 1950.

Hunt, James H. L. *Critical Essays of the Performers of the London Theatres.* London, 1807.

Jesse, J. Heneage. *Memoirs of the Life and Reign of George III.* 3 vols. London, 1867.

Jones, Claude E. "Dramatic Criticism in the *Critical Review,*" *MLQ,* June, 1959.

------. Ed. *Isaac Reed Diaries 1762-1804.* Berkeley, 1946.

Kelly, Hugh. *Thespis: or, A Critical Examination of the Merits of all the Principal Performers Belonging to Drury Lane Theatre.* London, 1766.

Kelly, John A. *German Visitors to English Theatres in the Eighteenth Century.* Princeton, 1936.

Lady's Magazine, The. London, 1770--.

Lichtenberg, Georg Christoph. *Lichtenberg's Visits to England. As Described in His Letters and Diaries.* Ed. and transl. Margaret L. Mare and W. H. Quarrell. Oxford, 1938.

Liesenfeld, Vincent J. *The Licensing Act of 1737.* Madison, Wis., 1984.

Literary Magazine, The. London, 1756.

Little, D. M. and Kahrl, G. M., eds. *The Letters of David Garrick.* 3 vols. Cambridge, Mass., 1963.

Lives of the Kings and Queens of England. Ed. Antonia Fraser. London, 1977.

London Chronicle, or, Universal Evening Post, The. London, 1757--.

London Evening Post, The. London, 1727--.

London Magazine; or, Gentleman's Monthly Intelligencer, The. London, 1732-85.

London Stage, 1660-1800, The, Parts 2, 3, 4, 5. Ed. Emmett L. Avery, Arthur H. Scouten, George Winchester Stone, Jr., and Charles Beecher Hogan. Carbondale, Ill., 1960-68.

Mitchell, Louis D. "Command Performances during the Reign of George II," *RECTR,* Second Series, I, i. 1986.

Monthly Review, The. Ed. E. Griffiths. London, 1749--.

Morning Chronicle and London Advertiser, The. London, 1769--.

Murphy, Arthur. *Gray's Inn Journal.* 2 vols. London, 1753-54.

Neville, Sylas. *The Diary of Sylas Neville, 1767-1788.* Ed. Basil Cozens-Hardy. Oxford, 1950.

Nicoll, Allardyce. *Eighteenth-Century Drama, 1700-50* and *1750-1800.* 2 vols. Cambridge, 1925, 1927.

Pedicord, Harry William. *The Theatrical Public in the Time of David Garrick.* New York, 1954.

Pittard, Joseph [Samuel Jackson Pratt]. *Observations on Mr. Garrick's Acting.* London, 1758.

Present State of the Stage in Great-Britain and Ireland. London, 1753.

Public Advertiser, The. London, 1752--.

Public Ledger, The. London, 1760--.

St. James's Chronicle; or, British Evening Post. London, 1761--.

St. James's Evening Post, London, 1755.

St. James's Magazine. London, 1762-64; 1774.

Sawyer, Paul. *The New Theatre in Lincoln's Inn Fields.* The Society for Theatre Research, London, 1979.

Schneider, Jr., Ben Ross. *Index to The London Stage 1660-1800.* Carbondale, Ill., 1979.

Sherwin, Oscar. *Uncorking Old Sherry.* London, 1960.

Stone, Jr., George Winchester, and George M. Kahrl, *David Garrick, A Critical Biography.* Carbondale, Ill., 1979.

"T. J." *Letter of Complaint to the Ingenious Author of a Treatise on the Passions.* London, 1747.

Theatrical Examiner, The. London, 1757.

Theatrical Monitor; or, The Green Room Laid Open, The. London, 1767--.

Theatrical Review; or, New Companion to the Playhouse, The. [John Potter]. 2 vols. London, 1772.

Town and Country Magazine, The. London, 1769--.

Troubridge, St. Vincent. *The Benefit System in the British Theatre.* The Society for Theatre Research, London, 1967.

Universal Magazine, The. London, October 1776.

Universal Museum, The. London, 1765.

Universal Visitor, The. London, 1756.

Weekly Magazine, The. London, 1760.

Westminster Magazine, The; or, The Pantheon of Taste. London, 1773-85.

Whitehall Evening Post, The. London, 1718-1800.

Wilkes, Thomas. *A General View of the Stage.* London, 1759.

Williams, John. *Children of Thespis, The.* 2nd ed. London, 1786.

Willson, Beckles. *George III as Man, Monarch and Statesman.* London, 1907.

Wortley Montague, Lady Mary. *Letters.* Ed. W. M. Thomas. 2 vols. London, 1861.